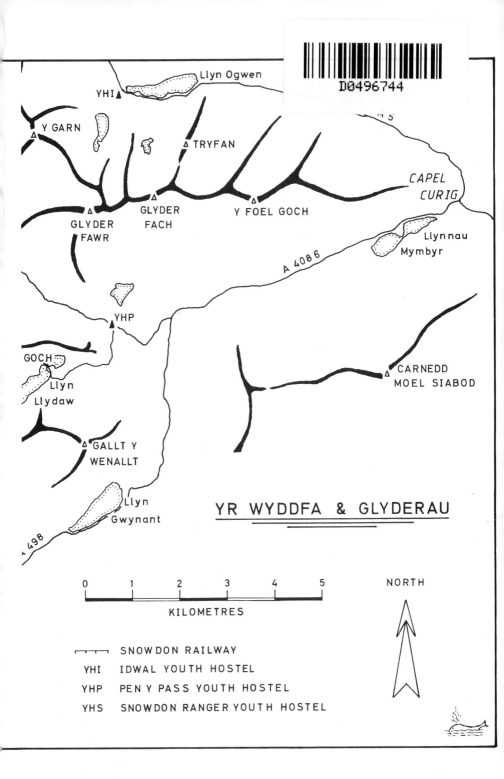

YR WYDDFA & GLYDERAU

Llyn Ogwen

YHI

Y GARN

TRYFAN

GLYDER FACH

Y FOEL GOCH

CAPEL CURIG

GLYDER FAWR

Llynnau Mymbyr

A 4086

YHP

GOCH

CARNEDD MOEL SIABOD

Llyn Llydaw

GALLT Y WENALLT

Llyn Gwynant

A 498

| 0 | 1 | 2 | 3 | 4 | 5 |

KILOMETRES

NORTH

SNOWDON RAILWAY
YHI   IDWAL YOUTH HOSTEL
YHP   PEN Y PASS YOUTH HOSTEL
YHS   SNOWDON RANGER YOUTH HOSTEL

Front cover picture: Harvey Lloyd

The Author with his SAR dog Gelert.

Geg Germany/Sunday Express Colour Magazine

COUNTDOWN

TO

RESCUE

Bob Maslen-Jones

 THE ERNEST PRESS

Published by The Ernest Press 1993

© Copyright Bob Maslen-Jones

Typeset by EMS Phototypesetting, Berwick upon Tweed.
Printed in Great Britain by St Edmundsbury Press Ltd.

A CIPP catalogue record for this book is available from the British Library.

ISBN 0-948153-22-9

Acknowledgements

I would like to thank my family and many friends for their help and
encouragement in writing this book.
In particular I wish to thank:–
Tony Jones for the maps;
Dewi Pritchard-Jones, H.M. Coroner for Eyri; for allowing me to research
his records;
All those who provided photographs from which I had to select but a few;
Those friends and relatives of climbers and walkers about whom the book
has been written, for their gracious understanding and acceptance of what I
have written.
The publishers would like to acknowledge the editorial work and supervision
of production by Mrs Margot Blyth.
Picture on page 148: "© Crown copyright 1992/MOD reproduced with the
permission of the Controller of HMSO".

CONTENTS

Foreword

This book has all the ingredients of a series of "thriller" detective stories, with the added fascination that the searches and rescues described by Bob Maslen-Jones are true, and related by a first-hand witness: – the author himself. There are numerous text books about safety in the mountains; the incidence of accidents is regularly recorded and analysed by competent mountaineering bodies. But such literature is, unfortunately, unlikely to be read by those with least experience of the risks which bad weather and difficult terrain represent, even in Snowdonia.

Herein lies the value of this book. For Mr Maslen-Jones has described in vivid, graphic writing what has happened (and will, I fear, continue to happen), when errors are made due to ignorance and foolhardiness which might, in many instances, have been avoided. But whether or not mishaps are avoidable, it is important that the splendid services provided by those who stand ready to search for, and rescue people who are reported as missing, should be better known and appreciated. The combination of skilled mountain rescue teams and their dogs with the helicopter pilots of the Royal Air Force, adds further flavour to these gripping stories.

I would add that accidents also happen to those of us who have enjoyed a life-time of experience as mountaineers. I have been a victim of two serious accidents, and two very near-escapes, in North Wales; and a number of others elsewhere in Britain, the Western Alps and the Himalayas. Such experiences, together with those of having joined rescue parties on several occasions, permit me to recommend "Countdown to Rescue" to everyone who ventures upon our mountains, and to many others besides.

John Hunt.

(Lord Hunt of Llanfairwaterdine)

Introduction

'Rescue' is an emotive word, but to the ordinary man-in-the-street a short news item in the Press or on TV that 'a climber has been brought to safety by the Llanberis (or other) Mountain Rescue team' means very little. The fact that many voluntary team members have spent a whole night on the mountain, struggling through deep snow or battling against storm-force winds and torrential rain or blizzards, and almost always at considerable risk to themselves, goes unmentioned.

In this book I have told the stories of many search and rescue incidents, mainly in the mountains of Snowdonia, as remembered by an ordinary person who was for almost fifteen years a member of the Llanberis Mountain Rescue Team (MRT), and with his search dogs Gwynne and Gelert in the Search and Rescue Dog Association (Wales). The variety of anecdotes in the book will fill in most of the gaps in the public's understanding of what really goes on when a group of men and women leave the warmth and comfort of their homes to go to the help of an unknown mountaineer or casual walker who is in distress, for no reward other than the satisfaction of having done so.

It makes a comprehensive and objective analysis of the cause and effect of each incident, and all the factual detail has been checked from coroners' and other records. The book is intended to be not only interesting reading for people who know little about mountaineering; it is also educational and should be of special value to teachers and leaders of young people on our mountains and moors. It is not intended to replace existing books about safety on mountains such as Eric Langmuir's 'Mountaincraft and Leadership', but to be read in conjunction with them so that the reader can relate the advice given – the 'rules of the game' – to what so often happens when those rules are not followed. I have tried to avoid direct criticism of any individual, but if there does appear to be any it is meant to be constructive so that others can learn from the mistakes described and hopefully lives will thereby be spared. We can all make mistakes, make the wrong decisions, or fail to react to a situation in the best way; and we all know how often we have been guilty of these shortcomings. But it is easy to be wise after the event, and I have set out the incidents in such a way that the reader can form his own judgement of where the main and subsidiary causes lay.

We are often asked why on earth we do it. There are two reasons; firstly, members of MRTs are the reason between somebody living or dying. There are many people alive and well today who were brought to safety by MRTs and who, without that quick and skilled response to a cry for help might well not have survived. Secondly, I am sure my colleagues in the rescue teams would agree with me when I say 'because there, but for the Grace of God, went I'. We have all at some time had a narrow escape, and it is our way of expressing our thankfulness that we were lucky and got away with it, that we follow the example of the good Samaritan and help others in trouble on the way. For, unlike the priest and the Levite, those in MRTs never pass by on the other side. To the casualty lying out there in the wilderness I commend the opening verse of the 121st psalm – 'I will lift up mine eyes unto the hills from whence cometh my help'. For that is where his help will come from – his fellow mountaineers.

KEY TO ABBREVIATIONS

chopper   affectionate slang for helicopter

km   kilometre(s)

km/h   kilometres per hour

LMRT   Llanberis Mountain Rescue Team

m   metre(s)

MR   Mountain Rescue

MRT   Mountain Rescue Team

NWMRA   North Wales Mountain Rescue Association

Oggie   Abbreviation of OVMRO and radio call-sign

OVMRO   Ogwen Valley MR Organisation

pt   point

RAMC   Royal Army Medical Corps

SAR   Search and Rescue

SARDA   Search and Rescue Dog Association

skip   skipper – adult leader of youth group

YTS   Youth Training Scheme

Dedication

For Anne
without whose whole-hearted and constant support,
co-operation and encouragement, my participation in
Mountain Rescue and the SARDA could not have happened.

The Beguiling Mountains

The screams of terror were carried away by the wind sweeping down from the ridge above . . . Roger watched in horror as his wife, Mary, hurtled down the mountain, the helpless figure leaving a trail in the smooth carpet of snow. His face whitened as he grasped his two sons . . . Suddenly their day out had turned into a nightmare. The mesmerically beautiful snow-covered mountain, glistening in the winter sunshine under a cloudless blue sky, had lured another unsuspecting family on to its treacherous slopes.

Seventeen-year-old Ben and his brother Tom, fifteen, were at home in Cheshire for their mid-February half-term break, and had suggested driving to Snowdonia on the Sunday to see the winter scenery. The weather forecast had warned that a front, carrying a lot of snow, was trying to push across Britain from the north-west, but that the high-pressure area centred over the North Sea would give way only slowly and the fine, bright and very cold conditions would probably last over the weekend.

Roger made a point of listening to the news and weather on every possible occasion – "In case I miss something important," he would say. So he heard the warning of a slow change in the weather and, at dinner on Friday, he suggested that if they were going to have a look at the mountains, perhaps it would be more sensible to go tomorrow – Saturday. Ben and Tom had other ideas. The Wales vs England rugby match in Cardiff was being televised live and nothing would tempt them to miss it. "Anyway, Dad," said Ben, "you don't want to believe all these weather prophets tell you. You worry too much". "Alright then, Ben, we'll go on Sunday but if it looks threatening we'll turn for home early. I'm not going to risk being snowed-up miles away in the mountains."

Sunday dawned cold and frosty, but the sun soon broke through the early haze. Mary prepared a picnic lunch and they set off in high spirits to see the white splendour of Snowdonia. Shortly before 11.00 a.m. they passed through Capel Curig and, looking westwards across the Mymbyr lakes, they saw the full beauty of the Snowdon Horse-shoe. As they drove along the valley towards Pen-y-Gwryd, the boys said they would like to abandon the plan to drive round the mountains and to climb Snowdon instead. It was such a lovely day, and they would have plenty of time to get to the top and back before dark. "How d'you know that?" asked Roger. "Well Dad," said spokesman Ben, "our outdoor-activities master at school comes up here a lot and he told me that anyone can climb to the summit and back in four and a half hours or so. There's a good well-marked path and the going's quite easy." "And what does 'or so' mean, Ben?" asked his mother. "Good point," said Roger, "what does it mean, Ben?" Doubt crept into Ben's voice as he said "Er, well, it means at least that time Dad, but we are all good walkers and if we can't do it, who can? If we park the car and get started, we can be back by 4 o'clock." It all seemed so clear-cut and easy. So easy that no-one thought about that weather forecast. No-one thought about the problem of finding their way safely off the mountain if conditions really turned against them. And no-one thought about the conditions on the path high up where the snow had been compacted by other walkers, thawed and re-frozen to form an ice-cap. Without crampons and ice-axes it would be difficult and very dangerous.

Roger's first reaction was to say "no". He knew little about mountaineering and felt uneasy about the idea, but allowed himself to be overruled. He knew they should not go up without proper clothing and equipment, but it looked so enticing that he thought it worth at least making a start and after all, they could always turn back. They found a space in the carpark at the top of the Pass and then, having asked the carpark attendant for advice – and he did not really have much idea about conditions on the mountain – they set off up the Pyg Track. It was just 11.30 a.m.

After walking steadily for an hour, they stopped for lunch, surrounded on all sides, except to the east, by high, rugged ridges. To the south-west, the paling sun was already past its zenith and high cloud had started to move in, diffusing the afternoon sunlight. It would not be long before the sun dropped behind the ridge. "I think we should get moving," said Roger. They had all begun to feel the chill mountain air and were glad to start walking again. Very soon the path became steeper and they found it increasingly difficult to keep their feet. It was already obvious that their footwear was totally unsuitable for the conditions – walking shoes or trainers are no substitute for proper mountaineering boots. Roger felt that maybe they should call it a day and turn back, but did not want to spoil his sons' enjoyment, nor to appear timid to them – to be an idol with feet of clay.

After another hour's walking, they struggled up the last pitch of The Zigzags, slipping and sliding on the steep, icy path. And then, suddenly, they were on the ridge. Just a few yards below them was the mountain railway line which would lead them to the summit, and beyond was a stupendous view across the foothills to Anglesey and Caernarfon Bay, the Irish Sea, and Ireland. The peaks of the Wicklow Mountains – eighty five miles away – were just visible. But, to the north-west, a menacing line of grey blotted out the horizon. For a few moments they gazed at this fantastic view which made all the effort of climbing up there worthwhile, and the grey cloud-bank went unnoticed. "Come on, Dad", said Ben, "let's get to the top, then we can go down. Mum looks cold."

Mum was indeed cold; she was also fairly tired, but was not going to be beaten by another ten minutes' walk and they all pressed on to the summit. After a few moments' rest, Roger felt a puff of cold wind and realised it was beginning to gust more strongly. He noticed, too, that it had swung round to the north-west where the grey line had crept a little nearer. A shiver went through his body – fear, or just cold? He realised again that none of them was wearing proper winter clothing, neither had they any spare jerseys, food or hot drinks with them. Other walkers nearby all seemed to have flasks, and many were already putting on extra clothing. He shivered again and said "Come on you lot, we're going down," and added "Now," as he saw Ben about to argue. As they reached the top of The Zigzags and started down, they knew it was going to be a slow and difficult descent. It is one thing to scramble up an icy slope, leaning into the mountain-side, but going down is different, as one's whole balance is altered, and the danger of slipping is much greater. All of them sensed that danger and were frightened.

Back on the summit, a Park warden called Simon had appeared and with a quiet but authoritative manner advised those still up there to make their way down as quickly and as carefully as they could. He told them he had just heard a warning on his radio that gale-force winds and heavy snow were imminent. "And that's it out there" he added, pointing towards the approaching cloud-bank. The wind was already blowing at force seven, and the sense of urgency in his voice had an immediate effect. As everyone started to get ready to move down, one of them told Simon "I think you may meet a problem going down; a family of four left here about ten minutes ago without any crampons or axes. In fact they were not even wearing boots and didn't seem to have much of a clue about anything. I reckon they'll be in trouble going down The Zigzags." "Thanks," said Simon, "that's all I need". It was something which happened again and again. "Why?" he asked himself, "why should I risk my life because people don't listen to advice and come up here in these conditions hopelessly ill-equipped?" "Oh well, I suppose I'd better go after them. Thanks anyway," he said. He smiled wryly

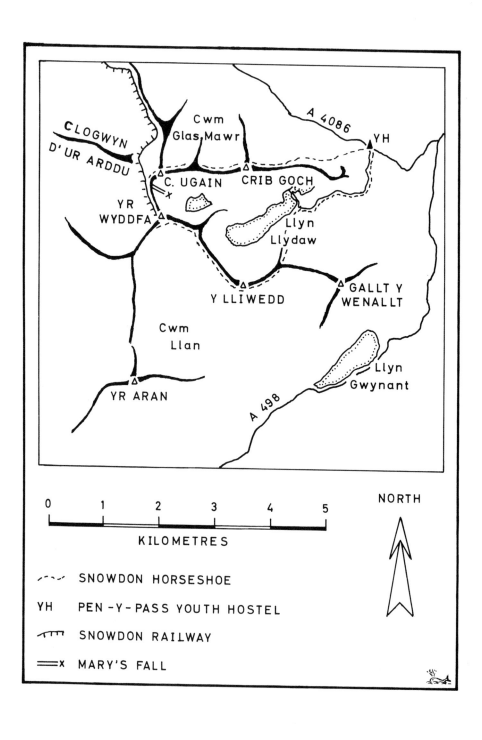

CLOGWYN D'UR ARDDU

Cwm Glas Mawr

A 4086

YH

C. UGAIN

CRIB GOCH

×

YR WYDDFA

Llyn Llydaw

Y LLIWEDD

GALLT Y WENALLT

Cwm Llan

Llyn Gwynant

YR ARAN

A 498

0   1   2   3   4   5

KILOMETRES

NORTH

- - - SNOWDON HORSESHOE

YH   PEN-Y-PASS YOUTH HOSTEL

SNOWDON RAILWAY

× MARY'S FALL

and walked swiftly towards The Zigzags. About 150 metres down the path, he saw Roger and his family making very slow progress, and he was just about to start down after them when it happened.

There was a ringing cry as Mary's feet slipped on a patch of ice. She slid off the path, heading down the steep slope. As she gathered momentum, she flailed her arms, trying desperately to stop herself, but she sped away leaving a track in the snow to mark the direction of her fall. Roger and the boys stood transfixed, as fear gripped them; fear for Mary, and fear for their own safety.

Mary had disappeared from their view as she slid below a shoulder of snow, but Simon saw her career past the bottom of The Zigzag path and come to a stop in a bank of soft snow just short of the next steep drop. She lay motionless about 250 metres below him, and must have been knocked out during her slide. She would almost certainly have sustained other injuries, probably serious ones, and help was needed urgently, especially with the blizzard closing in on them.

Simon shouted to Roger and others nearby to stay where they were. He would radio for help and then come down to them. Within a few minutes he had alerted police headquarters and asked for the mountain rescue team to be called out, and also suggested that the RAF search and rescue helicopter should be scrambled. It was only ten minutes' flying time away and he hoped they might be able to complete the rescue before the weather got too bad. Help was coming, and Simon made his way down to Roger and the boys who were all suffering from shock. He asked some of the other walkers nearby to walk them down past the bottom of The Zigzags to a point roughly level with where Mary was lying. Meantime the temperature had begun to drop, the sun had long since disappeared below the south-western ridge, and the sky had turned leaden.

Simon found Mary still lying motionless in the snow. She had a large bruise on her forehead and was unconscious but, as he carried out a quick examination, she stirred and was soon able to talk to him. As Simon continued with his examination, he found that both legs were broken, she had multiple bruises and abrasions, and clearly she was concussed; but thankfully she was still alive. It was important to keep her awake and talking, so Simon called Roger, Ben and Tom, who had just reached the point on the path nearest to Mary, across to see her. She was able to recognise them and they all experienced an immense wave of relief. Their worst fears, that she might have been killed in her headlong slide, had not been realised. Luckily the snow was deep enough to cover most of the rocks she might otherwise have crashed into.

With high ridges all round him, Simon had no radio communication with anyone, but he was sure help could not now be far away. He was a bit concerned about Ben and Tom, and he told Roger to send them down with their guides, or they would quickly become hypothermic standing around in the freezing wind. There was no choice, and Ben and Tom, now both very emotional, said goodbye to their mother and went on their way towards the carpark, some four kilometres away.

The weather was getting worse minute by minute and the first tentative flakes of snow were blown in on the wind. The distant sound of a helicopter's rotors coincided with Simon's radio crackling, and then the pilot came through loud and clear . . . "I have first-aid party on board and will drop them as near to your location as I can. I'll then return to your base to airlift the rest of the team. I'll stand by as long as I can, but may have to abort if the weather gets too bad." Simon acknowledged the message with relief; the long wait was nearly over and Mary and Roger clasped hands and just looked into each other's eyes without saying a word.

The helicopter came in and winched the three first-aid men down with the stretcher. They carried out essential treatment and immobilised Mary's legs in inflatable splints. Then they strapped her firmly to the stretcher ready for winching into the aircraft. The sound of the returning helicopter soon echoed round the rocky amphitheatre, but by now the cloud base had dropped below them and the pilot off-loaded the rescue team about 150 metres down the slope. They climbed up to where Mary lay on the stretcher and carried her to a position from which she was winched into the aircraft, and flown straight to hospital. It had been a race against time and weather and the rescuers had won.

As the helicopter disappeared into the darkening sky the rescue team relaxed, took out their flasks and drank some hot coffee. "Here," said Gareth, the team leader, as he handed Roger the first cupful, "you look as though you could do with this." "Thanks a lot, that's great," said Roger as he sipped the steaming liquid. Gareth offered him a Mars bar, always a sure stand-by for cold and tired walkers, and noticed how badly Roger was equipped and clothed for a winter expedition. But this was not the time to start lecturing him, and the priority was to get him safely off the hill and back to the carpark. He had been through a very traumatic experience and it was probable that some sort of reaction would soon set in.

"Well done, everyone," said Gareth, "that's two successful jobs today. Not bad at all. Let's go down then." The team members, tired but elated after a hard day, gathered up their equipment, checked it carefully, and headed off the mountain. Normally it would take about an hour to reach the road walking at a good steady pace, but the snow could not be far away and in ten minutes or so it would be almost dark. Perhaps an hour and a half would be more like it. Well before they reached the carpark the blizzard hit them and conditions became extremely severe. The youth hostel had opened its doors and provided hot drinks and sandwiches and everyone, now safely out of danger and acute discomfort, was glad to be inside. Roger found Ben and Tom well thawed out and in good spirits and, after saying their farewells and thank-you's all round, they drove away to Bangor while the Llanberis Pass road was still open.

Back in the hostel they were discussing the afternoon's events. "Well," said Simon, "it seems to me that you just can't win. You can advise, you can publicise the dangers, you can provide the most up-to-date weather forecasts but people, who in their ordinary surroundings are sensible and clear-minded, are mesmerised by the beguiling mountains and do stupid and irresponsible things. You can no more stop some people, ill-shod and ill-equipped, setting out on an inadequately-prepared expedition into the mountains, than you can persuade the motorway lemmings to slow down in fog. I'll tell you this though . . . that woman today was so damned lucky; when I watched her go over the edge I couldn't see how on earth she could come out of it alive. It was a miracle her head missed hitting the rocks, otherwise we'd have had yet another fatality in that area. It was sheer good luck that I happened to turn up when I did, for a bit more delay in getting the message through to the chopper and you chaps, and she wouldn't have stood a chance of being brought down until daylight. And in these conditions she wouldn't have lasted the night. Not a chance."

The story as I have told it is fiction, but is true in substance. It presents a scenario which is repeated in British mountains over and over again, year after year, and serves as a backdrop to what this book is all about. Not all incidents end in such happy circumstances, and it is a matter of luck whether the victim survives his fall, or the rescue operation becomes the recovery of a body. The story is intended to show how incidents often develop and, because of errors of judgement, escalate into disasters. It is also a matter of chance whether the RAF is able to scramble a helicopter. Sometimes they may be committed elsewhere in the mountains or out at sea, or the weather conditions or visibility may be too bad for them to operate; in either case the rescue then has to be carried out entirely by the mountain rescue teams (MRTs), and this is a very time-consuming job, often taking seven or eight hours or more, as the stories in this book relate.

Since I wrote this chapter, an almost copy-book incident, as far as the 'cause' goes, happened on Snowdon when a sensible and responsible father of two teenage boys was lured with his family on to the treacherous mountainside. They had intended to do only a short walk but, as adventurous boys are wont to do, the two lads forged ahead and soon lost contact with their parents. The route they were following on the south side of the Llanberis Pass is a relatively little used one, and after a while they wandered away from the path and found themselves on the steep rock-strewn slopes below Gyrn Las, where they split up. The younger boy chose a more difficult gully to the left of the main cliff, and they soon lost sight of each other. The elder boy continued to the ridge of Gyrn Las, waited for ten minutes, and then returned to the lay-by where they had parked their car, as he could get no response, either sight or sound, from his brother. After meeting up with his parents, they all searched for about an hour and a half, and at 4.45 p.m. they informed the police that the boy was missing. The Llanberis MRT was alerted and soon afterwards a full scale search involving the Search and Rescue Dog Association (SARDA) and MRTs was put into operation. It continued throughout the night but it was not until soon after dawn, at 7.40 a.m., that the crew of a Search and Rescue (SAR) helicopter spotted the missing boy at the foot of a 50 metre-high cliff. A member of the Llanberis MRT was winched down, only to confirm that it was the boy they were looking for and that he had been dead for several hours, having suffered very severe head injuries when he fell. The boy had last been seen alive at 1.20 p.m. by his brother. The weather was fine all day with little if any wind, but ground conditions, especially rock surfaces, were extremely greasy, due to a rainfall and low cloud earlier on.

The tragedy brings out a number of lessons, but perhaps the elder boy's statements to the coroner that, "it was a spur of the moment decision" (to go for a walk), and, "neither my brother nor I were suitably dressed for the mountains", really point to the primary causes. The media were quick to pick up the point, and the headline in the local paper the following day read 'Footwear folly of boy, 13, in hillside tragedy.' It told of the flexible, fur-lined 'moon boots' the boy had been wearing, which are normal wear indoors after a hard day on the ski slopes. They had no tread, and were totally unsuitable for use on the slippery and greasy mountainside. But apart from the boots, other lessons can be learned and should be heeded by anyone contemplating a walk in the hills. They are all covered in the course of the book, but to summarise them, they are:–

If you are not familiar with the area, always seek advice from someone qualified to give it, especially about safe routes, ground conditions and weather. Above all, keep to recognised footpaths. The obvious people to ask are the National Park wardens; that's what they are there for. Or the wardens of youth hostels or outdoor activity centres will always gladly help if you ask them.

Always keep your group together; never let it split up. If you do, you lose control straight away.

If a member of your group disappears, as happened in this incident, do not leave the immediate vicinity. Stay in the area and raise the alarm by shouting, waving or whistling. Try to bring help to you, rather than you leaving the site to summon assistance, because the odds are that once you do leave you will not remember where you last saw the missing person. It is vital for the rescue services to know as accurately as possible where to start looking. Otherwise a great deal of time will be needlessly wasted and the chances of the casualty's ultimate recovery greatly reduced.

Mountains need to be respected even by the most experienced mountaineers. They demand harsh retribution from anyone who acts irresponsibly and, unless people heed the lessons and warnings, there will continue to be shattered and grieving families as more and more people take to the hills. After all, the idea is to have fun and to come down safe and well at the end of the day. Learning the hard way may be too late as it was for this young boy, but if the lessons brought out by his tragic death are taken to heart, perhaps he will not have died entirely in vain.

I have to ask myself the question, however, how can we expect people from the towns and cities to be aware of the dangers? They see other people walking on the mountains, so why shouldn't they do so as well? It is not enough for mountain rescue people, or the police, to be quoted in the local papers week after week, urging visitors to the mountains to keep to recognised footpaths, and ask for advice, simply because those who do not know the area and are unaware of the hidden dangers of going into the mountains, do not read the local papers unless, perhaps, they happen to be staying in the area when the warning is published. And the same applies to warnings being broadcast on the radio or TV. Thus the message never gets through to those at whom it is directed. The father of the boy who lost his life in this tragic event suggested to me that if notices were displayed in carparks and lay-bys round the mountains warning casual visitors that, for example *"THESE MOUNTAINS CAN BE DANGEROUS. TAKE CARE, AND KEEP TO RECOGNISED FOOTPATHS"* fewer people would be lured into hazardous places. Certainly he himself would not have ventured away from the road if he had seen such a notice, and the tragedy would then not have happened.

The idea may be a good one, but to put it into practice would be an immense task. Around the Snowdon massif alone there are at least six main carparks, and probably three times that number of lay-bys. Then there are all the other popular mountain areas such as the Glyders, the Carneddau, the Moelwyns and Cader Idris to name but a few, so that the number of notices required to cover all possible 'holes in the net' would be enormous. How many of them would survive the depradations of vandals – yes, even in Snowdonia – is another question. For experience has shown that signs or plaques on the mountains are considered fair game to be destroyed. There must be a better way of trying to protect the people from the mountains, and the policy of protecting the mountains from the people by making the paths more pleasant and safer to walk on is obviously one of them. But the programme of path improvement on Snowdon, for example, is necessarily slow and ongoing and, anyway, will do nothing to stop people wandering on to grassy or rocky slopes where no path exists.

Weather Warning

' . . . and there will be strong to gale force winds over the mountains of North Wales . . . ' Not an unusual forecast, but for many people it is difficult to understand what it really means, and it is all too often ignored especially by occasional hill-walkers. Such a warning has serious implications, for wind can be a killer, particularly when, as so often happens, it blows up suddenly, catching walkers and climbers out on exposed crags and mountain tops. On a winter's day in 1986, every SAR dog team in North Wales was deployed on the ridges around the Ogwen Valley searching the cwms on the leeward side. There was a considerable amount of snow and ice on the hills, and a full gale had blown up quite suddenly during the morning when walkers had already reached the high ground. There were four separate incidents and in each case walkers had been blown off the ridge paths by violent gusts, ending up down the icy slopes of the cwms. Two of the incidents were fatal and the other two involved stretcher rescues as the wind was too strong and turbulent for the SAR helicopters to assist.

Experienced walkers listen carefully to weather forecasts and take note. If there is any likelihood of a gale springing up, they adjust their routes to avoid exposed and narrow ridges. Sometimes an unusually violent gust can be heard approaching like an express train – a 'screaming banshee' – and when it arrives it can last a minute or two. Those who have been hit by one of these screamers waste no time in hitting the deck and grabbing anything solid to avoid becoming airborne. The first time I experienced such a wind my two dogs were almost swept away and I threw myself to the ground and grabbed them both just in time. We lay there hugging the earth, the dogs shaking with fright until the gust had passed on.

Many people who have never been caught in a storm in the mountains deliberately go out to experience the force of Nature in one of its angry moods. I did so myself in my younger days, but it is really rather a foolhardy thing to do. And yet, until people appreciate how dangerous it is to be high up, exposed to storm-force winds, it is understandable that they want to see for themselves.

At about noon on Sunday December 1st 1985, three students, Iain Thornton, John Glazebrook and Lloyd Hadlington, set out to walk up the

North Ridge of Tryfan via the Heather Terrace, where they would be on the lee side of the mountain. As forecast, the wind speed had increased during the morning and shortly before leaving the lower part of the North Ridge to get on to the terrace, the boys stopped for a rest. Iain and John remained standing whilst Lloyd sat down amongst some rocks. It was still raining at this time, but the strongly gusting winds seemed to have died down. However, as they were getting ready to move on, there was a sudden and violent gust. Iain and John were both lifted bodily into the air and blown clear of the ridge, coming to rest amongst boulders some way down the slope.

As soon as the gust had passed over, Lloyd made his way down to where his friends were lying on the scree, to find Iain apparently dead, and John seriously injured and shouting for help. He had hurt his legs and back. There was little Lloyd could do for them, and the priority must be to get expert help. He went down to the valley to alert the rescue service and at 1.00 p.m. the police were informed of the incident.

There happened to be a party from the Ogwen Valley Mountain Rescue Organisation (OVMRO) not far away on Tryfan and they were directed to the accident site by radio, reaching the casualties at 1.30 p.m. This group had also been struck by the same freak gust and some of them too had been blown off their feet.

The weather leading up to the accident had been much as forecast with continuing heavy rain and very strong gusty winds from the south and south-west. The speed of gusts recorded at RAF Valley between 11.30 a.m. and 12.30 p.m. that day was up to 35mph, and of course this figure would be considerably greater on the mountains.

The cause of the accident must surely be attributed to bad luck that Iain and John were standing up when, without warning, they were picked up and blown off the mountain. If there was any secondary cause it could only be that perhaps the boys were a bit over-ambitious and in the forecast conditions their choice of route was not too wise. But that is again conjecture. It was a matter of gaining more experience, and if climbers and walkers are going to wrap themselves in cotton wool, they will never learn anything.

The cause of Iain's death was due to cerebral lacerations from fractures of the skull, and it was suggested that if he had been wearing a helmet perhaps his head injuries would not have been so severe. But how many hill-walkers normally wear helmets? Rock climbing is a different matter but to suggest that everyone going on the hill should insure themselves against every

Spindrift being blown off the north ridge of Crib Goch, with storm clouds over Snowdon.   *John Roberts*

eventuality, is sheer fantasy. John himself recovered from his back injuries, which included three broken vertebrae.

Without practical experience of wind strengths, theoretical knowledge must be the next best thing, and a chart of the Beaufort scale of wind force is given on the next page. It gives a clear indication of the sort of damage which can be inflicted by the varying degrees of wind speed and particular note should be taken where it states that 'walking is difficult'. Even away from exposed ridges, wind can be a serious problem to contend with as it gusts in powerful eddies down from the high tops. On one occasion I was walking down the Pyg Track from Snowdon when I was hit in the back by a sudden violent gust and was propelled forwards, crashing into a large boulder at the side of the path. I suffered a badly bruised and very painful knee, but if the boulder had not been just there, I would have been away down the slope and this book might never have been written.

THE BEAUFORT SCALE OF WIND FORCE

Force	Description	Wind Speed		Effect inland
		mph	km/h	
0	Calm	0	0	Smoke rises vertically
1	Light air	1-3	3-6	Smoke drifts gently
2	Light breeze	4-7	7-12	Leaves rustle
3	Gentle breeze	8-12	13-19	Leaves, rushes, grass move; light flags extended
4	Moderate	13-18	20-29	Raises dust and paper
5	Fresh	19-24	30-39	Crested wavelets on lakes; small trees sway
6	Strong	25-31	40-50	Wind whistles in crags; large waves & spray blown off lakes
7	Moderate gale	32-38	51-61	Difficult to walk against the wind
8	Gale	39-46	62-74	Very hard to walk into the wind; special care with wind gusting from behind & sides
9	Strong gale	47-54	75-87	Almost impossible to walk; some damage to buildings
10	Storm	55-63	88-101	Difficult to stand; safer on hands & knees; danger of being blown off paths; seek shelter
11	Violent storm	64-82	102-131	Impossible to stand; widespread damage to buildings, trees, pylons etc.
12	Hurricane	83+	132+	Disaster everywhere

Dissent on the Mountain

February 1978. It had been a fine day, the mountains glistening with frozen snow and ice. The wind had turned into the north-west towards the end of the afternoon, and the forecast was for more heavy snow showers before morning. In the hotel we had a full-house and dinners had been served when the telephone rang. Anne had just taken the staff to their homes, so I took the call. There was an incident, and I was asked to report at the Snowdon Ranger Youth Hostel, some seven miles away, as soon as possible. I asked the guests to look after themselves in the bar, and to 'slate' anything they wanted! Then I changed into my mountain gear, made myself a flask of coffee, left a message for Anne telling her what had happened, and was on my way.

This was my first big job with the Llanberis MRT (LMRT), and as I drove up the Nant-y-Betws to the hostel, adrenalin was coursing through my body with the excitement and apprehension. On arrival at the Snowdon Ranger Youth Hostel we were briefed as follows: 'A lady in her mid-fifties, a member of a mountaineering club from the Home Counties, was missing somewhere on the west side of Snowdon. She had been with a party from her club which had set out to climb Snowdon from the youth hostel. At the top of the Snowdon Ranger Path zigzags, they found conditions very slippery with iced-up footpaths and, as they were equipped only for normal hill-walking with no crampons or ice-axes, the leader wisely decided to abort the expedition and turn back. This did not please the lady in question who, incidentally, had only recently joined the club. She protested that she had never climbed Snowdon, and was not going to miss the chance now. The summit seemed very close in the clear air, but the leader stood firm and was backed up by his other members. Short of physically restraining her there was no way of stopping the lady and the leader told her that if she was not back at their base by 8.00 p.m., she would be reported overdue.

The lady went on her way and, when she reached the railway line, walked a short way towards the summit before deciding to leave her rucksack by the line and walk to the summit and back without it. There seemed to be no-one else on the mountain and, in spite of the ice and snow, she achieved her

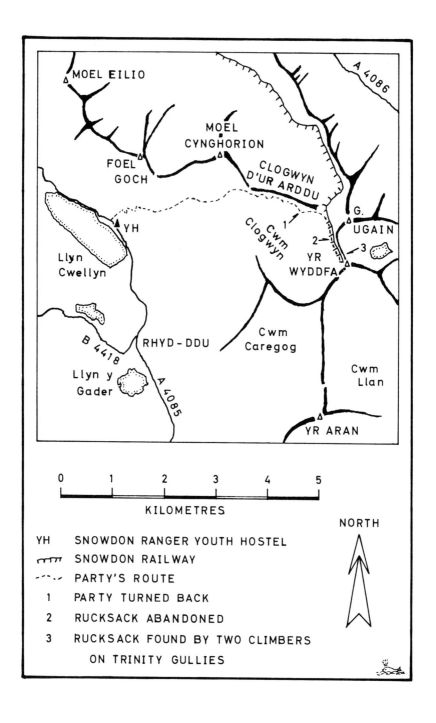

MOEL EILIO

MOEL CYNGHORION

FOEL GOCH

CLOGWYN D'UR ARDDU

A 4086

YH

Llyn Cwellyn

Cwm Clogwyn

G. UGAIN

1

2

3

YR WYDDFA

RHYD-DDU

Cwm Caregog

Cwm Llan

B 4418

A 4085

Llyn y Gader

YR ARAN

```
0    1    2    3    4    5
KILOMETRES
```

NORTH

YH   SNOWDON RANGER YOUTH HOSTEL

⌐⌐⌐   SNOWDON RAILWAY

- - -   PARTY'S ROUTE

1   PARTY TURNED BACK

2   RUCKSACK ABANDONED

3   RUCKSACK FOUND BY TWO CLIMBERS
     ON TRINITY GULLIES

objective. However, just as she disappeared up the track alongside the railway line, two climbers came over the ridge from Central Trinity Gully on Clogwyn-y-Garnedd and saw her rucksack. They looked inside and found it contained map, compass, food, flask and clothing. Their immediate thoughts were that it belonged to a walker who had become hypothermic and, in the mental confusion which accompanies exposure, had discarded it. They took it with all speed down to the road, and thence to the police station in Llanberis.

What happened to the lady when she found her rucksack had gone was never clearly established. Suffice it to say that she had not rejoined her party by 8.00 p.m. and that the leader reported her missing to the police. As they already had her rucksack, the police feared she had come to some harm and, as the area where she had disappeared was fairly small and accurately known, the LMRT was called out to mount an immediate search using only 'ground searchers'. The forecast of snow before morning weighed heavily in the decision to do everything possible while the weather remained fine and clear.

I was asked to accompany two team members, Gwynfor Williams and Cledwyn Jones, both of whom were in the Gwynedd Ambulance service, to walk up the Snowdon Ranger Path to the plateau above The Zigzags and search as widely as possible, compatible with our own safety, on both sides of the path. It was one of the most beautiful nights I can remember; clear and still – the calm before the storm – with a slight breath of cold air from the north-west touching our cheeks. From high up, we could see a vast pattern of lights spreading out from Caernarfon down in the valley, to north and south, and away to Holyhead on the far side of Anglesey.

We found nothing, and at 2.30 a.m. we were recalled to the search base at the youth hostel and told to be ready for a further search at daybreak. Since it was still only 3.15 a.m., I decided to go back to the hotel, get something hot inside me, and tell Anne what was going on. It was my turn as breakfast chef and she would have to stand-in for me! I found her asleep in bed, book on her chest, and having explained things to her I had a cup of hot chocolate and a bowl of cornflakes. I refilled my flask, said good-bye, and went out to the car. During the half-hour I had been in the hotel, there had been a heavy snowfall, leaving four inches of fresh snow on the ground. Somehow I managed to slither back to the youth hostel and had an hour's sleep on a hard bench before the briefing for my second ascent to the plateau within eight hours.

I was paired with Leo Taylor, an experienced British Mountain Guide,

Llyn Ffynnon y Gwas and on the left Clogwyn d'ur Arddu, with the Snowdon Ranger Path zig-zagging up the ridge. To the right is Cwm Clogwyn, backed by the cliffs below snow-covered Snowdon, South ridge and Llechog ridge. This view also illustrates the route taken by the Scouts in the lead story in chapter 19.   *Author*

had not been out on the search during the night, and from the start I was aware that he was much fresher than I was! We reached the top of The Zigzags where ground conditions were much different to what they had been a few hours earlier, and we donned crampons. The snow was deep and soft, but on the plateau itself the north-westerly wind, which had increased to 'very strong', was whipping up spindrift and creating blizzard-like conditions. Although it was no longer snowing, the general conditions, unlike the previous night, were extremely cold and unpleasant.

Our task was to contour from near the top of The Zigzags, skirting Cwm Clogwyn above the cliffs below the summit of Snowdon, as far as the Llechog ridge. We had just started the traverse and, as we moved through the crags and around buttresses, I heard a metallic 'clank'. I looked towards Leo and saw him somersaulting down the steep snow-covered slope. It all happened very quickly and there was nothing I could do except stand, spellbound, and watch. After his third somersault he threw out his legs to form a triangular base, and this effectively stopped his 'Gadarene' rush to disaster. It was a cool, premeditated action if ever I saw one, and I hurried over to Leo and found him entirely unmoved. "My bloody crampon strap broke," he said as he re-fixed it with a spare boot-lace. Some guy, I reckoned.

Shortly after daybreak, an RAF helicopter began a precise search of the crags below us, methodically moving up and down, very close to the cliffs, and traversing slowly the hillside. At 8.30 a.m. Leo received a message over his radio for us to stay where we were until a party from the RAF Valley MRT joined us. There was no sign of them at this stage, so we sat down on the bare hillside, and decided to have some coffee and sandwiches. There was no shelter from the blown snow and freezing wind, and I soon began to feel cold. In spite of buttoning up to the neck, the spindrift managed to find its way inside and made life very uncomfortable. My coffee cooled so quickly that it was only luke-warm by the time I reached the bottom of the cup.

The thought of continuing the search with the RAF lads seemed less and less appealing as we sat and waited for them, and a slight panic began to develop as I realised that my exertions during the first part of the night, added to lack of sleep, had caught up with me and I was fast running out of steam. I recognised the first signs of hypothermia in my condition, and tried to fight them off by convincing myself that this could not be happening to me. By 9.00 a.m., I knew I had to tell Leo that I had had enough, but I did not have the guts. How could I fail on my very first operation with the team? I would never live it down. In retrospect, the fact that I did not face up to the inevitable was just another sign that hypothermia had me firmly in its grip, and I was no longer fully in control of my thoughts and actions as my condition deteriorated.

I remember looking at my watch again as the Valley men approached. It was 9.10 a.m. and I had begun to feel really ill. My coffee had long since been finished, and I was just about to call it a day when Leo's radio crackled . . . "the missing person has turned up safe and well. All rescue personnel return to base." The RAF lads had just joined us, and they radioed the helicopter for a lift down to the base area.

Member of the LMRT belayed on Crib Goch ridge, ready to assist another team member being winched down.   *Harvey Lloyd*

They walked across the icy slope to where the helicopter was hovering and, as they were being winched into the aircraft, we followed them over. I had never been in a Wessex helicopter before, and I had no firm idea how to put the strop on!

However, somehow I made it without falling out, and seldom have I experienced such a feeling of relief as when I sat down in the helicopter. We were soon down at the youth hostel where a most welcome breakfast, courtesy of Dave Woods, the warden, was waiting for us. Before I left for home to catch up on my lost sleep, I caught a glimpse of the 'missing lady' who looked remarkably clean and tidy and well-rested for someone who claimed to have been wandering around the mountain all night. I never heard what had really happened to her, but her Club was most contrite for her behaviour, and made a generous donation towards the team's funds, whilst the lady herself had her membership promptly terminated.

The incident highlights the importance of discipline amongst hill-walking parties, largely composed of inexperienced people but with an experienced leader. It must be of a high standard, and all members should understand and accept that the decisions of the leader are binding on everyone. The lady was guilty of putting her own ambition before the interests of the rest of her party; and, as it turned out, before the safety of the large number of people who turned out to look for her.

As far as my own efforts were concerned, I learned a salutary lesson – that stamina is not inexhaustible. Since this incident, I have twice been involved in mountain-top rescues after being on the summits within the previous eight hours and on each occasion I ended up utterly exhausted. I have also learned that 'pride comes before a fall'. There is a lesson here for group leaders no less than for individuals, for there is nothing cowardly about turning back when it becomes clear that the prudent thing to do is to abort the expedition and head for lower, safer ground and home. Whether this is because of the condition of a member of the group, or of the weather or ground, is immaterial; the responsible hill-walker knows when he or she should turn back, and must be prepared to do so before it is too late. There is always another day.

Billy Robertson-Jones Search

On Sunday October 13th 1980, I had already gone to bed when the 'phone rang. It was just after 11.00 p.m. and Jesse James, the team leader, asked me if I could be available for a search at first light. "Yes, I can," I said, "what's the story?" He told me that the assistant-warden of the Snowdon Ranger Youth Hostel was last seen leaving the hostel in climbing gear just after midday. He was alone, and the person who saw him go did not notice which direction he took. He had been due back in time to open the hostel at 5.00 p.m., but when he had not turned up two hours later, Dave Woods, the warden, reported him missing to the police and the Llanberis MRT was asked to help.

It seemed an awful long time – twelve hours to be exact – between 7.00 p.m. and first light, and I asked Jesse whether any search dogs were being deployed. In all fairness, very little was known at this time by rescue teams about the use and potential of trained search dogs, and after a short discussion Jesse said he would telephone SARDA and ring me back. This he did some fifty minutes later, and asked me to be at the youth hostel at 4.00 a.m. with my dog, Gwynne. I confirmed that I would be there, and asked what other information he could give me. "He's called Billy Robertson-Jones, twenty-one years old, and is known to be a hard climber who does a lot of soloing. But we've got no idea at all where he might have gone," Jesse replied. "So rather than dissipate our ground resources on a 'needle-in-a-haystack' search at night we will put in two dog teams, you and Arthur Clarke, to do Cloggy and Cwm du'r Arddu. Arthur will meet you at the hostel at 4.00 a.m. The main search will begin soon after dawn, giving you three hours' start, by which time hopefully we may have picked up one or two clues. If he has been seen somewhere, we can concentrate our efforts in that area and with luck wrap it all up fairly quickly. As he went out in climbing gear, it must be a reasonable bet that he headed for a not-too-distant crag. He would be limited by time, so can't have gone very far, and the most likely place seems to me to be Cwm du'r Arddu below Cloggy. If we draw a blank there, we can eliminate it from further searching..'

Like all dog handlers who have spent a great deal of time training for such an event, I was excited that at last Gwynne and I were going out in earnest and not just on another exercise – I was extremely keen to get out there. Arthur Clarke and his dog 'Baggins', a very experienced team, were waiting for me at the rendezvous as arranged and, after a few minutes spent getting ready and discussing the situation, we started up the Snowdon Ranger Path towards Snowdon. Our plan was to search the area between the road and the north and south ridges of Snowdon. We would begin halfway up the mountain at Bwlch Brwynog and do the rest of the area back towards the road after we had searched the crags and higher ground. Arthur set off to the north to cover the whole of Cwm du'r Arddu as far as Clogwyn station, and I took the other side of the Ranger Path through Cwm Clogwyn right round under Snowdon to the Llechog ridge.

By 7.45 a.m. considerable radio traffic had built up, and soon small groups carrying out sweep searches appeared here and there, scattered all over the vast area. Many of them were covering the area I had already searched with Gwynne, which highlighted the lack of confidence in the ability of the search dogs! When I had completed all the steep and rocky sections of the cwm, I dropped down to the flatter and less interesting ground and found myself thinking as much about how to get the SARDA message across, as about the actual job I was doing. I was sure Billy would be found somewhere near a climbing crag and not on the wide-open grassy slopes of Nant-y-Betws which we were searching, but the plan to work outwards from the last sighting was perfectly correct, and the whole area had to be cleared, with no stone left unturned.

The operation built up quickly, and Billy's father and brother, Stuart, and many volunteers joined the search. Gwynne and I carried on until 11.30 a.m., which was an unbroken stint of seven hours. She was still working well when we returned to the hostel for a rest and, after feeding her, I put her in the car to sleep, while I enjoyed a very welcome breakfast provided by the hostel. There was still no further information about Billy's possible whereabouts and, at about 2.00 p.m., we joined a search party on Mynydd Mawr across Llyn Cwellyn. Both Gwynne and I were tired and I withdrew to be ready, if necessary, for a further search during the night. In any case to be part of a sweep search was not the proper use of a search dog, as all the human scents only confuse the animal. Dogs should always be used in isloation as we had been during our first stint.

There is an ad hoc group called the Search Panel which consists of representatives of the North Wales Police, the North Wales Mountain Rescue Association (NWMRA), and all teams and organisations, such as the

Craig y Bera seen across Llyn y Dywarchen.   *John Roberts*

RAF SAR Helicopter flight, taking part in an operation. During the early stages of a search the organisation and control is the responsibility of the MRT involved, but if and when the searchers have drawn a blank and the number of people on the ground and the size of the search area have become so big that the leader feels that it is getting too much for him to handle, he may ask for the Search Panel to assemble. This brings fresh minds to the problem and also means that everyone involved is represented in future planning and all their ideas can be considered.

In this incident the Panel, chaired by Tony Jones, OVMRO, was called in about mid-afternoon. Tony also represented the North Wales MR Association as its secretary, the Llanberis MRT was represented by John Ellis Roberts, and C flight, 122 Squadron RAF, by Flight-Lieutenant Alan Coy. By this time the Llanberis MRT had been joined by RAF Valley MRT, members of the Ogwen Valley MRT and an increasing number of volunteers. Two helicopters from C flight were operational throughout the day, during which time the search area had been extended into the Moel Hebog and Cwm Pennant areas, and along the Nantlle ridge to Cwm Silyn.

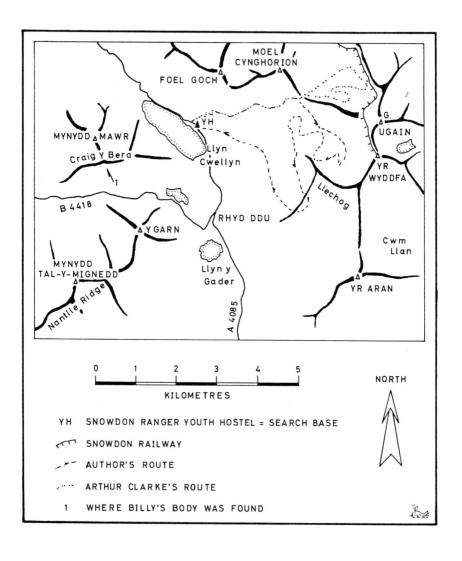

MOEL CYNGHORION

FOEL GOCH

MYNYDD MAWR

Craig Y Bera

YH

Llyn Cwellyn

G. UGAIN

YR WYDDFA

1

B 4418

Llechog

Y GARN

RHYD DDU

MYNYDD TAL-Y-MIGNEDD

Llyn y Gader

Cwm Llan

Nantlle Ridge

A 4085

YR ARAN

| 0 | 1 | 2 | 3 | 4 | 5 |

KILOMETRES

NORTH

YH   SNOWDON RANGER YOUTH HOSTEL = SEARCH BASE

SNOWDON RAILWAY

AUTHOR'S ROUTE

ARTHUR CLARKE'S ROUTE

1   WHERE BILLY'S BODY WAS FOUND

By the end of the day it covered over a hundred square kilometres. The weather had been fine but was already deteriorating and there was little the Panel could do other than plan operations for the following morning. There was still no information, and Billy seemed to have vanished into thin air. At dusk, rain and low cloud had settled in and everyone was recalled for regrouping and rest.

The search had been given a lot of publicity on the TV news bulletins during the day, and the first breakthrough came in the early evening when some people in the Midlands who had been walking on the Nantlle ridge on the Sunday afternoon, telephoned the North Wales Police to report that they had seen a lone climber in what looked like a rugby shirt in the area of Craig-y-Bera at about 4.00 p.m. The Panel now had something to work on, and planned to send in the RAF Valley team to search the area as soon as the weather improved sufficiently. During the latter part of the night, the hoped-for break occurred and at first light the search was resumed. It was not long before the RAF team found Billy lying at the foot of Craig-y-Bera, but he had already been dead for several hours. He had suffered severe injuries; and it seemed certain that he had died from hypothermia and shock due to internal bleeding during Sunday night – before the search for him had started.

The main lesson to be learned from this sad incident is that Billy should have told someone responsible where he was going. It was a classic example of what can happen when climbers or walkers go into remote areas without leaving a route-card. This does not have to be elaborate; it can be just a few words written on a slip of paper or even a verbal message. Too many people habitually fail to follow this sensible routine, firmly believing that 'it will never happen to me.' But it does, far too often, and a little forethought in leaving word with someone who will raise the alarm and tell the police where to start looking if you become overdue, will save the rescue services a great deal of time, effort and risk, and furthermore will enhance your own chances of survival if you have been unlucky enough to have had a serious accident. Billy was not one of these people; he had been working at Snowdon Ranger Youth Hostel for some time and, until the unlucky 13th of October, he had always told the warden where he was going and what he intended to do. It is 'Sod's Law' that on the one occasion when he failed to do so, he fell and injured himself so seriously that he succumbed before anyone knew where to go to help him.

It is thirteen years since Billy Robertson-Jones died on the mountain, and during that time the Search and Rescue Dogs have 'come of age' and all progressive MRTs now ask SARDA for help at the outset rather than grudgingly calling them in as a last resort, when all else has failed. Ten years or more ago, a search meant deploying large numbers of men in long lines to carry out sweep searches across an area. It was rather a hit and miss affair, especially at night or in bad visibility, when a searcher literally has to walk over a casualty, or pass so close to him that he can not fail to see him. Someone lying between two searchers, possibly buried under a blanket of snow, or in a heather hollow, could certainly be missed. The study of search techniques was then in its infancy so that, with the knowledge and experience available at the time of the incident, no-one involved in running this particular operation can be blamed for the delay in finding Billy. He could have been anywhere, and Craig-y-Bera was not then, and is not now, one of the popular climbing crags.

With the benefit of hindsight and the improvements in search techniques, when a search of this sort is mounted today, all available dog teams are called out immediately and are deployed to cover the most likely areas. Whether in the Billy Robertson-Jones incident Craig-y-Bera would have been included as one of these, no-one can say; it would depend on the search manager, his knowledge of the whole surrounding area, and all the information and clues he has managed to collect. As dogs were not a considered option, however, and in the circumstances at the time, the decision not to deploy any ground searchers until daylight must have been right. The ability of human beings to search rough ground at night is limited even with a powerful hand-lamp, and it would have been a wasteful and rather pointless use of the manpower resources available.

Loner on Lliwedd

On July 8th 1981, a sixty-year-old major in the Salvation Army, on holiday in Nant Gwynant, left the hostel where he was staying at about 9.30 a.m., saying that he was going to do a route solo on the East Buttress of Lliwedd, and would be back in time for supper. But when the other hostel guests sat down for the evening meal, there was an empty place. Hoping that he had only been delayed, the warden had his meal kept for him and, as is the normal practice, he waited two hours after his expected time of return, in case his lateness was due to some minor mishap. When there was still no sign of the Major by 9.30 p.m., the warden reported him missing to the police.

Eight members of the Llanberis MRT, including three SARDA handlers and four dogs, started searching the area between Llyn Llydaw and the base of the Lliwedd crags at 11.00 p.m. The three dog teams were myself and Gwynne, Heather Maling and Bramble, and Roland Layland with two dogs, Wensley and Bluey. The wind was blowing from the south-west and we were almost completely sheltered by the cliffs of Lliwedd, towering 450 metres above us.

Each dog team was allocated an area to search, with Heather at the eastern end, me in the centre, and Roland to the west. We worked our way along the side of the lake to our allotted areas, and began moving across and upwards towards the base of the crags. The five ground searchers from the team were to do a line search from east to west when the dogs had completed their search, and they waited in the wings until signalled forward.

At this time some of us were experimenting with working two dogs at the same time and, on this search across fairly broken ground, I could not see how a handler could possibly watch two dogs which might be well apart from each other. It was not long before my doubts were confirmed. Roland's two dogs were ranging widely, and it would have been impossible for him to watch them both carefully enough to notice a possible indication. At precisely ten minutes after midnight, forty minutes after we had started the search, I was watching Gwynne working across the base of a scree towards Roland's area when I saw a 'cold light' moving right to left across my front.

North face of Lliwedd from Crib Goch. The East Buttress is on the extreme left of the cliff.
The search area covered all the ground between the path (left) and the rocky spur (right), from
the lakeside to the foot of the crags.   *Tony Welch*

(A cold light is a plastic illumination stick giving off a bright green/yellow light, which we attach to the top of the dog's search coat at night). The light reached the bottom of the scree immediately below East Buttress and shot about two hundred feet up the steep scree like an elevator. Suddenly it stopped and I listened for the tell-tale bark which would indicate a find. But none came.

After a short time Roland shouted across to me "Have you seen Bluey, Bob?" "Yes," I said, "he's about two hundred feet above you just below East Buttress, and sitting motionless." "Got him," he said and was off after him. I called Gwynne and followed up the scree, certain that Bluey had made a find, studiously ignoring Roland's request to bring his rucksack which he had discarded in favour of more speed. One rucksack was enough for me to carry!

As Roland drew near to Bluey, who was still motionless, he called out that he thought we had the missing man. The fact that Bluey had not 'spoken' to indicate his find is quite common when our dogs find someone who is already dead. The dogs are taught to 'speak' on finding, but they seem to sense when it is too late, and remain sitting beside the deceased person, completely mute. Bluey had indeed found our missing man, who had been dead for some hours. Rigor mortis had set in, and he was in a kneeling position, head in his hands, propped up amongst the boulders close in to the crag. It seemed from his position that he must have been in great abdominal pain as he died, and we were all very saddened by what we had found. His climbing rope was wrapped round his body, and his grey/green clothing was very difficult to see amongst the boulders of the same colour. It was a matter of conjecture whether he would have been found by line searchers unless one of them had walked right over him. The fact is that a search dog had picked up his scent within forty-five minutes, and the search was over.

This was the first time any of the five ground searchers had seen search dogs working, and although they all admitted that it had been a very impressive and spectacular performance, one member said that they would have found the man anyway within a very short time. So once again prejudice was seen to be dying hard. As far as working two dogs together goes, this incident proved that it cannot be done. The likelihood of a handler missing the vital indication is too great, and SARDA (Wales) subsequently made a rule that handlers will not work more than one dog at a time on an operational search.

Once again the risks of climbing alone were obvious. One can only guess what happened to the Major, but Roland climbed the same route next day and found an old piton which it seemed likely the dead man had tried to use as a belay. He was probably tired and perhaps failed to tie on properly, and fell about 30 metres. When climbing solo, there can be only one mistake; there are no second chances.

The Babes on the Mountain

Our long, unremitting battle to establish the Search and Rescue Dog Association's credibility received a tremendous boost towards the end of October 1982 when a night-long search for two small children ended in success just before dawn. Not only had it been a classic search operation, it was also given very wide publicity in the national newspapers and on television and at last our dogs were given their correct title of search dog, and not tracker or sniffer dogs. It may seem a matter of little importance, but in SARDA we had been trying for a long time to get it right!

It all started when the two children, Catherine, 11, and Julian, 12, got bored sitting in their holiday cottage near Nant Peris at the foot of the Llanberis Pass. They sat looking at the steep-sided 600-metre Llechog ridge across the narrow valley, and the challenge it presented gradually became too much for them. They put on their anoraks and wellingtons and told their mother they were going for a short walk. It was just after 3.30 p.m., and she told them to be back in time for tea. They set out, relieved that Mum had not asked where they were going.

When they did not turn up at supper-time both parents were worried. The father, who was a keen hill-walker and realised that it would be like looking for a needle in a haystack as they had no idea in which direction the children had gone, informed the police in Llanberis straightaway. After they had checked the cafés and roads in and around Llanberis without result, the police asked the MRT to help, and John Ellis Roberts telephoned me and asked for four SARDA dog teams to report at the base in Nant Peris as soon as possible. I received this call at 8.15 p.m. and passed the call-out message to Roland Layland, Phil Benbow and Heather Maling. Phil Williams-Jones, chairman of SARDA, happened to be with me in the hotel at the time, and he felt certain that unless the children were found very quickly, there would soon be a call for every other available dog team in North Wales. He returned to his home in Conwy, and put all remaining dogs on stand-by.

The four dog teams were deployed by 9.15 p.m., and the Llanberis team was called out to do in-filling line searches. The strategy was to work outwards from Nant Peris in the hope of finding the children quickly.

40

The Llechog ridge on the south side of the Llanberis Pass at Nant Peris. Clogwyn Clwyd
Gully is in the centre of the picture.   *Author*

We had considered the possibility that Catherine and Julian might have
sneaked up the steep slope onto Llechog ridge, but thought it most unlikely
that even if they had tried, they would have got very high up. While two of
the dog teams were committed to the north of the road, Roland and I were to
work our dogs on the south, or Llechog ridge, side. I took the western end of
the Pass and Roland searched as far as Blaenant and up into Cwm Glas Fach
and Cwm Glas Mawr.

   Gwynne and I crossed the river at SH 604583 and worked from the
track/road junction at 598587 along the river bank to the stream junction at
614575, gradually moving up the slope which became ever steeper until,
above the mountain wall, the going got very slow and difficult. The wind had
increased in strength and was blowing from the north-north-west diagonally
across the slope, which created problems in working the dogs effectively.
Parts of my area were very rough, and in particular the woods close to the left
boundary were wet, slippery and loose underfoot, and required great care.

   By 11.00 p.m. the call for extra dogs had been received by Phil Williams-
Jones, and it was not long before they were all operational. The search area
was increased to accommodate them, and now included the Llanberis path
and railway line from Llanberis to the summit of Snowdon to the south, and
the Glyders, Elidir Fawr, Foel Goch and Y Garn to the north.

At 3.30 a.m. there was still no sign of the children and there had been no indication whatsoever from any of the dogs. John decided to recall the searchers to rest, and to restart the operation at 7.00 a.m. From midnight onwards there had been about a hundred people out on the mountain but as the search area expanded, more and more searchers would be required, and John intended to ask the Ogwen Valley, Clwyd and RAF Valley MRTs for help. It is usual when children's lives are at risk to 'pull out all the stops' and that is what John was doing now. In addition to the ground searchers he was asking for, he had already laid on the helicopter from C flight to over-fly the area as soon as it was light enough.

I went home to bed to try to get some sleep before the re-start at 7.00 a.m., but I was aware that one dog handler, Phil Benbow, had offered to do another search from Clogwyn station (SH 607562) directly into the wind along the Llechog ridge as far as the Clogwyn Clwyd gully at 600576, and Hugh Davies had volunteered to go with him as navigator. Phil had to be at work at 9.00 a.m. and offered to do this extra stint as he would not be able to make a worthwhile contribution at 7.00 a.m. So as the rest of us went home, Phil and Hugh, with search dog Jet, made their way to Clogwyn station and then toward the base at Nant Peris, where John Ellis Roberts remained operational.

There had been no indication from Jet, and when they reached Clogwyn Clwyd they decided to call it a day and scramble down the gully to Nant Peris. They had gone down about 15 metres when Phil suddenly noticed that Jet was not with them. He called and whistled but there was no response. "He must have found" said Phil, more in hope than with conviction. "We'll have to climb back up and see where he has gone." Back on the ridge Phil called and whistled again, but there was still no answer. He calculated that the best bet would be to look for Jet upwind from where he had last seen him. This would take them diagonally down the slope away from the gully on to very steep ground which would require extreme care. Before long Phil spotted Jet's red fluorescent coat in the beam of his hand-lamp and slowly and carefully moved down to him. There, lying in a scooped-out hollow under a rock, were the two cold and frightened children.

The scent from the children had been blown up on to the ridge and Jet must have picked it up just as Phil and Hugh had started their descent. He followed it to the children about 50 metres away and sat guarding them until Phil came down to him. Catherine and Julian were well enough to be walked off the mountain down to Llanberis and were soon re-united with their parents over a dish of hot soup and were able to tell their story.

When they had reached the really steep ground, they looked down and realised it would be too dangerous to go back down. They were afraid of losing their balance and falling, so they kept on climbing, sticking their penknives into the ground like mini-ice-axes to help get a hold. Julian planned to reach the ridge, drop down to the railway line on the other side, then walk to the police station in the village. But darkness overtook them just before they reached the top and they were lucky to find a sheltered spot under a boulder where they could get some protection from the wind. Here they crouched and cuddled each other to try to keep warm, but it was too cold and they spent a miserable night until they eventually fell asleep from sheer exhaustion. Fortunately it was dry and they came to no harm, but if it had turned wet and they had not been found for three or four more hours, it might well have been a different story.

I was fast asleep when John Ellis Roberts telephoned to say that the search was over. Anne answered the phone to hear John describe the event as "a classic find by search dogs" which was very gratifying to say the least. John was well-qualified to judge, as in the very early days of SARDA he had two German Shepherd search dogs and had some very good finds himself.

Subsequently, because of all the national publicity about 'The Babes on the Mountain', Jet was awarded the PRO-DOGS Gold medal for devotion to duty, which was well deserved. Phil and Jet had already searched an area to the north of the Llanberis Pass before they began their extra stint along the Llechog ridge, and were on the mountain for seven and a half hours before Jet picked up the children's scent.

The Pack Leader

I still have a pair of Gortex overtrousers which bear the patched scars created during a memorable and, for me, a most unpleasant night in February 1983. We had been called out at around 9.00 p.m. to search for two climbers who had set out to climb a route on the Idwal Slabs, then to walk up to Glyder Fawr and return down the Gribin to Ogwen Cottage, where they expected to arrive at 5.00 p.m. There was a lot of snow high up, and there were formidable cornices on the north side of the Glyder plateau.

Short, token searches had been carried out by the Ogwen Valley team around the Slabs and lower part of the Gribin up to the snow line, but when no sign of the two men had been found, SARDA was called in to search overnight, leaving the Ogwen Valley team to carry on at daylight if they were still missing. Phil Benbow and I were detailed to work closely together to cover the ground from the top of the Devil's Kitchen to Glyder Fawr, then to follow the route the two climbers had intended to take, i.e. down the Gribin ridge. For some reason I had both my dogs, Gwynne and Gelert, with me that night, in spite of the rule that only one dog could be worked at one time. There must have been a good reason and, as I remember, Phil was quite happy about it.

As we walked up the path to the top of the 'Kitchen', I was not feeling my usual ebullient self and I suspected that I was in for a stomach upset. However, I pressed on and by the time we reached the summit of Glyder Fawr I was feeling very unwell and my stomach seemed to be turning to water. My discomfort was not helped by the weather; the wind was blowing almost at gale force and sweeping hail, sleet and snow horizontally across the plateau. It was one of those times when conditions could justly be called 'atrocious', a turn of phrase much liked by journalists.

As we worked our way up on to the plateau from Llyn-y-Cwn and across the flat top of the Glyders, all three dogs appeared to pick up snatches of scent every now and then, but not strong enough to follow up. It was likely that the wind was driving the snow into their nostrils and reducing their scenting efficiency. Nevertheless, it was encouraging and we both felt that our two climbers must have passed along our route a short time before, and

Llyn Idwal with Idwal slabs (left) and the Devil's Kitchen (right of centre).   *Tony Welch*

were probably not too far away. From Glyder Fawr we turned in the direction of the Gribin ridge on a compass bearing, and there we found a massive cornice blocking the way down, with no sign of anyone having cut through it. We decided to work our way along the edge of the plateau above Nameless Cwm to Castell-y-Gwynt in case the men had managed to find a way off. But it was all undisturbed cornice and there was nowhere we could get down that way either. As the wind was blowing from the south we were happy that if there was anyone anywhere on the plateau to our right, the dogs would have picked up their scent and homed-in on them. So the whole of Glyder Fawr had effectively been covered and we were free to move on.

It was now about 2.30 a.m. and my nausea was getting very much worse. I began to feel a slight panic as we continued through the snow-covered boulders around Glyder Fach, and we agreed to find a way down on the south side into less unpleasant conditions. But wherever we tried we were penned in by menacing cornices, and shortly before 4.00 a.m. I realised that I was nearing the end of my energy reserves. "Phil" I said, "I've got to shelter up until daylight. I feel really ill and unless I stop now, you're going to have a real casualty on your hands." Phil had not realised how bad I had

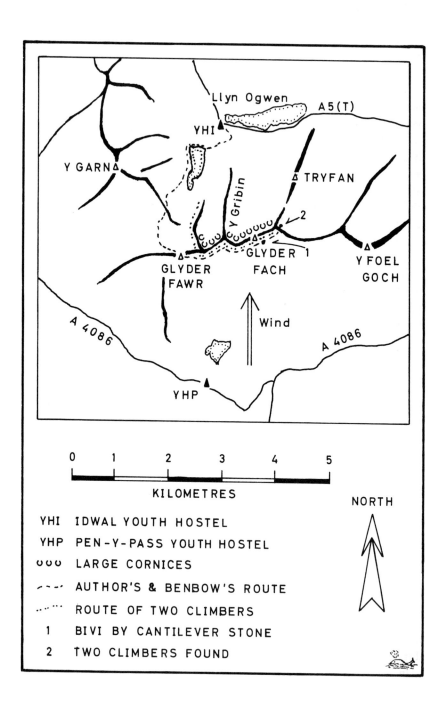

KILOMETRES

NORTH

YHI   IDWAL YOUTH HOSTEL
YHP   PEN-Y-PASS YOUTH HOSTEL
ᴗᴗᴗ   LARGE CORNICES
-‑-‑‑ AUTHOR'S & BENBOW'S ROUTE
.··‥   ROUTE OF TWO CLIMBERS
1   BIVI BY CANTILEVER STONE
2   TWO CLIMBERS FOUND

become, simply because I had hoped it would all go away and I had not told him. Of course, with hindsight it was crazy to try to go on, feeling as I did. I still had not learned the lesson from the search on Snowdon in 1978!

We found a sheltered place under some rocks near the Cantilever Stone, and I got into my sleeping bag. But not for long. Within ten minutes I had to get out and rush off – downwind – and get rid of what was troubling me. It was a close run thing and to have to take off jerseys and salopettes in a near blizzard, with time fast running out, is something I shall never forget. I never want to experience the like of it again. But all was well and immediately afterwards I began to feel better. I went back to my sleeping bag, but did not risk getting into it again and lay with it over me, and soon felt much more comfortable.

At this stage Phil said he would try to get communications with Phil Williams-Jones who was manning the base set at Bryn Poeth, the Ogwen Valley MR Centre, as we had lost touch with him several hours earlier. He went out into the storm and headed towards Bristly Ridge at the end of the plateau, leaving his dog, Jet, a big, strong and heavy Labrador, with me. At once, he curled up across my legs and went to sleep. I called to my two dogs to come and lie down as well, but all they would do was to come and lick my face and go out again. I had not given them much thought when I first lay down in my sleeping bag, but I now saw that they were circling slowly round and round the shelter, and realised that I was witnessing the pack instinct at work. A dog's master is always his pack leader as he is the one who looks after the dog, provides food and gives out the orders. In this situation, Jet could not have cared less about me except that he no doubt appreciated the warmth he was getting from my legs. But Gwynne, the older of my two dogs and therefore in front as they circled round me, and Gelert, taking second place, were protecting their leader – me! No matter how much I tried to get them to come under the boulder, I could not get them to desert their post.

Five minutes after he had left me Phil managed to get radio contact with base and he reported that he was very concerned about my condition. I heard what he was saying on my own radio and felt most embarrassed. How are the mighty fallen! According to Phil I was very ill, and "he had got me in a sleeping bag in a sheltered position near the Cantilever Stone." Base promised to get two members of the Ogwen Valley team to contact us and help us off the hill as soon as it was light, assuming that I was able to walk. By now I was feeling stronger and knew I could get myself down without much difficulty. I was improving rapidly and even drank some hot coffee.

In the meantime, after acknowledging the last message from base, Phil heard something rustling nearby. He shone his lamp around and saw two figures asleep in the rocks behind him. They were the missing climbers. It transpired that they had tried to find a way off the Glyders just as we had, and in the end they had found themselves on Bristly Ridge and decided it was too dangerous to attempt to descend in the dark as they only had small hand torches with them.

This did not go down in the records as a SARDA find, although if I had not become ill, we would not have found them as we had no intention of trying to descend Bristly Ridge. I heard Phil report that he had got the two men, and I then waited for him to come back to the shelter. As he led them across the plateau to our position, Gwynne and Gelert would not let them come near. Their protective instincts lasted until I went out and called them off, but even then, although they knew Phil well enough, they continued to growl. It was the two strange men who upset them.

As soon as it was light enough to see, the two 'guides' joined up with us and led us down the steepest slope I have ever tried to descend without a rope. There was no path, just a vestige of a sheep track here and there and, with legs still weak from the effects of my ghastly night, I found it very difficult to get myself safely down and I must have sat and slid as often as I stood and walked. It was not my normal method of descending a slope, but in these rather exceptional circumstances I am not ashamed to admit it.

Down below, the shape of a lake became more distinct and I soon recognised it as Llyn Bochlwyd, the outline of which is strangely similar to the map of Australia. The route we were following was very steep, and is normally only tackled upwards as a snow and ice climb! Thankfully we all got down safely without mishap, except to my overtrousers, and walked back to base and a hot drink.

Avalanche

In SARDA (Wales) our philosophy has always been that our dogs teams should be able to answer a call for help anywhere, at any time. And that means being able to work effectively in virtually any situation. Since the Welsh mountains are free of snow for the greater part of the year, and avalanches are a rare occurrence compared with Scotland, many people not immediately concerned with the search dogs opined that it would be a waste of time trying to train them for avalanche conditions. We took a very different view, feeling that if there should be a call-out to search for an avalanche victim, we must be able to deal with it properly.

In February 1984 a party of four climbers with experience of snow and ice climbing in Scotland and the Alps was swept a thousand feet down the Black Ladders in the Carneddau by a huge avalanche. Two of the party survived with only minor injuries, but their companions were both killed. The location of the incident was known to within a very few metres, and the Ogwen valley MRT and a SAR helicopter from Valley quickly recovered the two bodies and SARDA was not involved. But contrary to what our critics had said, at last there was fresh evidence that big avalanches can and do happen in the Welsh mountains and SARDA's credibility received a boost.

It was not long before another avalanche occurred; this time in Sinister Gully in Cwm Glas, in January 1985. Two climbers were caught and swept down about 170 metres into the cwm. One of them survived, but the other was buried under the debris and was killed. By the time the survivor managed to get down to the road and raise the alarm, it would almost certainly have been too late, even if the buried climber had not been killed during the fall, and again a helicopter recovered his body.

The following year, on January 28th 1986, two students from Bangor University, Marcus Pither and Stephen Payne, aged twenty-three and twenty respectively, set off at 7.00 a.m. to do *The Somme* route on Ysgolion Duon (The Black Ladders). Both climbers were well clothed and properly equipped for winter mountaineering, and were experienced and proficient under normal conditions, though Stephen had done only a little snow and ice work. There were several inches of fresh snow on the mountains and for the first part of the day more snow fell at intervals, with bright periods between times; however, during the morning the snow showers became more frequent, often merging into continuous snowfall. At about midday a friend of the two climbers, Paul Owen, saw them at an estimated 100 metres up the cliff and they appeared to be making good progress. Soon afterwards a large avalanche was reported on an adjacent route, *Ice-fall Gully*, but subsequently another friend, Noel Crane, heard voices which he identified as those of Marcus and Stephen. They were in cloud, but their voices were unmistakeable. There were then no further sightings or sounds of them.

Marcus and Stephen had arranged to telephone Paul Owen at 6.00 p.m., but no call came and at 9.30 p.m., after making local enquiries, he informed the police. He asked, however, that no action be taken until he and some of his friends had carried out a search up Cwm Llafar to the base of Ysgolion Duon, and while they were doing this, stand-by messages were sent to the Ogwen Valley team (Tony Jones), SARDA (Phil Williams-Jones), and others likely to be involved if the token search being carried out by the friends of the missing climbers drew a blank. In worsening weather with low cloud and poor visibility Paul and his colleagues found conditions extremely difficult. By midnight they had found no trace of the two men, and they requested all possible help from the rescue services.

Dr Tony Jones, a demonstrator in Marine Science at Bangor University, who has for many years devoted a great deal of his time and effort toward developing search and rescue techniques in Britain, set up a search management team (of which I, as SARDA call-out co-ordinator, was a member) in his flat in Bangor. From here he could get excellent line-of-sight communications into the head of Cwm Llafar and the Ysgolion Duon area, and also with the 'Oggie' team base at Bryn Poeth in the Ogwen Valley.

Three dog teams were called out immediately, namely Roland Layland, Phil Benbow and Roger Pyves, and each had a navigator with him. The task was to walk up Cwm Llafar and search the area of highest probability around the base of Ysgolion Duon. They were on the mountain soon after midnight and confirmed that search conditions were very difficult indeed. There was fresh snow on the ground to a depth of more than a metre and it was still snowing heavily with very poor visibility.

Although we feared that the missing men had almost certainly been avalanched sometime during the afternoon, it was possible that they had managed to finish their route and had tried to walk out over the summit of Carnedd Dafydd and make their way down to Ogwen Cottage. We therefore deployed three more dog teams and navigators to cover the most likely routes

John Hulse in the equipment room at Oggie Base. John assisted Tony Jones as co-ordinator throughout the avalanche incident. He is a member of OVMRO of long standing.   *Tony Jones*

from the Ogwen Valley to Carnedd Dafydd. The first dog teams had arrived at the head of Cwm Llafar and reported a large avalanche cone (field of avalanche debris) at the bottom of Ysgolion Duon. They worked systematically over the whole of this area with a few rather indeterminate indications from the dogs until 6.00 a.m. when they decided to pull out for a rest.

In addition to the 'Oggie' team members, the RAF Valley MRT had been called in to help, and a party of fourteen of the most experienced avalanche searchers from both the 'Oggie' and RAF teams, led by Roger Jones and equipped with avalanche probes, shovels and the normal rescue gear, was to set out from Gerlan, on the eastern outskirts of Bethesda, at dawn. A further party was to be held in reserve in Bangor. Hugh Walton, leader of the Llanberis MRT, had heard the 7.00 a.m. Radio Wales News bulletin, and telephoned to offer help from his team. As we already had a reserve group held waiting to be deployed, Tony decided not to accept Hugh's offer immediately, but we were all agreed that if there was still no sign of Marcus and Stephen by 10.00 a.m., we would ask him to provide as much help as he could raise from his team.

While Roger Jones's party was moving to Gerlan, Roger Pyves radioed in to say that dawn was breaking, it had stopped snowing and the weather was clearing. In fact they could see Bethesda and the cloud was lifting rapidly. He also told us that they could now identify the extent of the avalanche cone which had been partially obscured by the heavy overnight snowfall. Shortly after this message was sent, the three dog teams resumed the search of the cone. A request for a helicopter to overfly the area and closely examine the Ysgolion Duon immediately above the avalanche cone, with Tony as observer, had been agreed, commencing at 9.00 a.m.

At about 8.30 a.m., Phil Benbow's dog, Jet, scented and dug out a red rucksack. A short distance away, in line towards the cliffs, Roland's dog, Toby, found a mitten buried under the snow, and within five minutes Roger's dog, Dusty, working up the same line, found the first of the two men under a foot of snow. The search continued and, as the helicopter approached, the dog handlers requested the pilot not to come any closer to the cone as the down-draught would whip up spindrift from the fresh snow and make it impossible for the dogs to continue scenting. The aircraft landed away from the search area, Tony got out to take control on the ground, and the helicopter took off again for Gerlan to pick up Roger Jones's party and airlift them into the cone area. While this was going on, Roger Pyves and Dusty had searched from where they had found the first climber up the slope to the foot of the crags, where Dusty quickly found the second body buried about a metre under a huge pile of snow. After returning to Gerlan with Roger Jones and his men, the helicopter then came back to pick up Tony and the two bodies and fly them to hospital in Bangor.

All the SARDA teams and other search personnel were recalled and were off the mountain by 11.30 a.m., and the search was over, less than twelve hours after it had begun. As he declared the incident closed, Tony said, "Well, if any one still had any doubts about the value of SARDA, this must dispel them for good. Without these dog teams it could well have taken us two or three days to find the two bodies." It had been a classic search operation, and in SARDA we felt that at last we had 'come of age' and had been accepted. Tony had been one of the hardest nuts to crack for a long time, and what he said was high praise indeed. From the point of view of the way the whole operation was planned, with members of Tony's 'Oggie' team each taking on a specific responsibility, it had worked extremely well, and since then the whole concept of the planning and execution of searches has been developed still further on the basis of search management teams.

A Miracle on a Mountain

Early on New Year's Day 1986 an experienced hill-walker, Robert John Hughes, took his ten-year-old daughter, Jillian, for a day-long expedition on the Carneddau. He left his Land-rover at Trasbwll (SH 732663), and arranged to telephone his wife when they came off the mountain at 6.00 p.m. Their planned route was to follow the track from Trasbwll to Melynllyn, then up the ridge to the refuge on Foel Grach, and to return down the line of the footpath into Cwm Eigiau and back to Trasbwll. By 8.00 p.m. his wife had not heard from him and she informed the police. Ogwen Valley MRT was informed and initially four dog teams, each with a navigator from 'Oggie', were deployed on the mountain.

The peaks and ridges had a fair covering of snow and ice, and conditions were far from suitable for a ten-year-old to be taken high up. Neither Mr Hughes nor Jillian had crampons or ice-axes, but they did have walking-sticks, good boots and plenty of warm clothing. They also had a good supply of food and hot drinks. During the morning the weather deteriorated, as predicted by the Met Office, and there was considerable snowfall creating a virtual white-out. It seems that they failed to find the refuge hut and, after walking round and round for some time trying to find it, headed down towards Cwm Eigiau – or so they thought. In fact, the pair had not headed down into Cwm Eigiau, but were 180 degrees off course and were somewhere to the west of Foel Grach when they decided to get what shelter they could amongst the iced-up boulders. It was a long and very cold night.

In the words of Robert Hughes, "We were on completely the opposite side of the mountain to what I thought." But, even without the use of a compass, the strong easterly wind which had been blowing all day 'down the back of his neck', should have been blowing almost directly into his face if he had turned to go down the east side of Foel Grach into Eigiau. With the wind blowing from behind, an experienced walker should have realised that, unless the wind had changed, he was going in the wrong direction, i.e. towards the west. But the clue went unnoticed.

When the search began, three dog teams were deployed to cover the whole of the intended route as already described. This route was entirely to

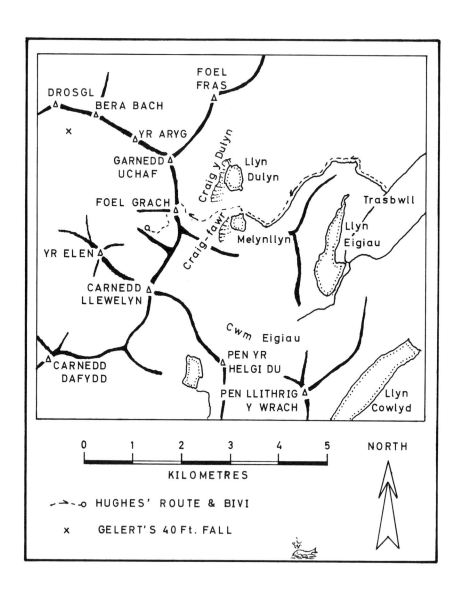

DROSGL △
BERA BACH △

×

YR ARYG △

GARNEDD
UCHAF △

FOEL
FRAS △

Craig y Dulyn

Llyn
Dulyn

FOEL GRACH △

a

Craig-faw

Melynllyn

Trasbwll

Llyn
Eigiau

YR ELEN △

CARNEDD △
LLEWELYN

CARNEDD △
DAFYDD

Cwm Eigiau

PEN YR △
HELGI DU

PEN LLITHRIG △
Y WRACH

Llyn
Cowlyd

0   1   2   3   4   5

KILOMETRES

NORTH

- ->-o HUGHES' ROUTE & BIVI

×   GELERT'S 40 Ft. FALL

the east of the Foel Grach ridge. One dog team, myself and Gelert, with Doug Jones as navigator, set off from Bethesda to search the area along the Afon Caseg up to Llyn Caseg and Afon Wen. As we found out later, it was on the steep ground above Llyn Caseg that the missing pair were sheltering.

At about midnight Doug Jones suggested that we should have a look at a small, disused quarry just to the left of the path. I sent Gelert in and, as he responded to my command, he suddenly disappeared. A second later I heard a sickening crunch and one pathetic cry. Then silence. Immediately in front of me I could see the dark shadow of an unfenced quarry hole, and we peered over the edge shining our hand-lamps, trying to see the poor dog, who had fallen fully 12 metres on to the rocks below. I felt sick, and was frightened that Gelert was dead. I only vaguely heard Doug saying that he used to play in the quarry as a boy and that there used to be a tunnel into the bottom of the quarry hole. Before I realised what he was doing he ran off, saying "I'll see if I can find it." I still could not see Gelert, but after about three minutes I heard some movement and he staggered into the beam of my lamp, very unsteady on his feet. I thought that if he could stand and even walk, he must have escaped serious injury and a tremendous wave of relief went through me. I just wanted to get him out of that hole.

Doug had managed to get through the old tunnel, and as he called to Gelert I saw the dog turn and lurch towards him. He followed Doug along the fifty metres of flooded tunnel through which Doug had crawled to rescue him. It was a selfless and brave thing to do. I went back towards where I reckoned the tunnel entrance would be and as Gelert came out, he could not even raise a wag of his tail. He collapsed on the snow which quickly turned crimson from the many cuts he had suffered.

Happily the dog was not seriously hurt. He had broken teeth, concussion and multiple cuts and abrasions and was in deep shock; but the snow proved too cold for him and he was soon on his feet and we walked him slowly back to the roadhead. In the meantime I had radioed the news through to base at Bryn Poeth where Phil Williams-Jones arranged for a 'half-stretcher' party to come out to help get Gelert down, and he also sent in another dog team to take over the area I had been searching. As we reached the road, we met four men with one half of a Thomas stretcher on their way to help us, but there was by then no need for them and they somewhat disappointedly returned to Bryn Poeth. It would have been an unusual rescue in which to have taken part, carrying an injured dog off the mountain! The incident of course underlines the risks search dogs so willingly undertake when they are working in the dark. It was not the first accident suffered by our dogs 'in action', but fortunately, so far, none of them have resulted in serious injury or death. I am most grateful to Doug Jones for his immediate action, at considerable personal risk, to rescue Gelert, and I shall not easily forget it.

High up in the icy crags the weather had deteriorated and the wind was gusting strongly, increasing the wind-chill effect. The father and daughter, who were both deeply religious and dedicated members of their local church, carried out the correct survival routine. At intervals they drank some soup or hot chocolate and ate sandwiches, chocolate biscuits or cake to maintain their body warmth. "We tried to cat-nap, but it was too cold to sleep and we kept shouting for help and flashing our little torch," said the father. "I was very frightened and thought we were going to die," he went on, and his daughter added "and throughout the night we kept singing hymns to Jesus and hugging each other to keep cheerful". In the meantime the search on the eastern side of Foel Grach ridge went on. The mountain refuge was buried under a huge snow drift, and there was no sign of the two missing walkers in any of the likely sheltering places such as disused quarry buildings or shelter stones.

On the western side, the dog team which had taken over my search area was given a slightly different task a little to the south, and they, too, found nothing. As it turned out, their revised area did not include the crags where

The mountain refuge below the summit of Foel Grach almost covered by a snowdrift.   *Author*

the walkers were sheltering. The wind was ideal for searching throughout the night and I am convinced that if Gelert had not come to grief he would have picked up the air scent from the missing people and chalked up another find for SARDA.

By the middle of the night the RAF Valley MRT were deployed to do a line search along the ridges between Trasbwll and Foel Grach. The Llanberis and Clwyd teams, with more reinforcements from 'Oggie' and a helicopter from 122 Squadron, joined the search early on January 2nd and an increasing flow of volunteers swelled the number of searchers during the day. Every available search dog was now on the hill and I had rejoined the search with Gwynne. The operation was still concentrated on the east side and no further search was carried out from Bethesda. This was because someone staying in a cottage in Cwm Eigiau reported having seen the ten-year-old girl making her way down towards the Conwy Valley during the afternoon of January 1st. If it was her, it was thought that her father must have had an accident or been taken ill and was almost certain to be lying out there somewhere on the eastern side of the mountain. And what had happened to the little girl who had not been seen subsequently? The entire search effort was now concentrated in this extensive area and was for two people who had apparently become separated. In fact this turned out to be false information and whoever the girl was, seen walking towards the Conwy Valley, she was not the one for whom we were looking. But the search organiser was not to know this until the end of the day.

Up in their sub-zero shelter, Robert and Jillian decided to try to get down to lower ground and at about 8.00 a.m. on January 2nd they set off. A fierce gust of wind hurled them off their feet soon after they started, slightly injuring them both. He sprained his ankle, and the little girl pulled a muscle in her leg. In their fall they lost a rucksack and one of their walking sticks which went careering out of sight down amongst the icy crags, and there was no way they could recover them.

The weather had again deteriorated with snow and fog, visibility being reduced to as little as fifteen metres. By midday, with still no sign of the missing walkers, hopes were rapidly diminishing, but the search went on and shortly before dusk a helicopter rejoined the operation and overflew the lower part of Cwm Eigiau. In the meantime father and daughter had found a stream which they thought would lead down to Llyn Eigiau, and throughout the day they struggled over very difficult ground through the fog. Progress was painfully slow, but then, as the fog lifted (which allowed the helicopter to resume flying on the other side of the mountain) they saw some lights in the distance. They followed them until they reached an isolated farmhouse on the outskirts of Bethesda, and the incident was at an end.

During the next few days there was a great deal of criticism of Robert Hughes for taking his young daughter into the very severe conditions prevailing, and failing to navigate properly. A letter to the editor of the Liverpool Daily Post (Welsh edition) was published in which Mr Hughes was criticised for getting lost. The writer pointed out that had he carried the appropriate map and a compass, and been familiar with their use, then they would not have been lost. Mr Hughes replied to this letter agreeing completely with what was written. He said that he did have a map and compass with him, but that, having been in that area so many times, he relied on his own judgement in trying to reach the refuge which he thought was close. He wrote "I should have stopped and taken a compass reading before the mist became so thick. Later it was too late to do that as I did not know exactly where we were. A map and compass are of use only if one knows where one is to begin with. Fell-walkers should never make my mistake, but rely on their maps and compass . . . " With which I entirely agree, having made precisely the same mistake myself so many years ago. Like Mr Hughes we got away with it, but only just.

Was it a miracle on a mountain as the headline of the Daily Post proclaimed? As far as the missing pair was concerned, it certainly was; they are convinced that they had been delivered safely from their ordeal, and that, to save them from spending another night out in the bitter cold, they had been sent a guiding light. But what is a miracle? Is it an event due to super-natural power as Mr Hughes and his daughter believed, or is it, in its more commonplace context, an unusual or remarkable event? The fact that they survived in freezing temperatures may well be the miracle to which the headline referred. But whilst being relieved and thankful that they were safely delivered off the mountain, we should think of the many other unseen miracles which occurred during this operation. That over one hundred people were ready and willing to get out of bed in the middle of the night, or leave their work and lose their livelihood while out on the mountain, and go out into the icy and often dangerous conditions to look for the missing couple, is surely a remarkable event? And they do it voluntarily. They would not have it otherwise.

Amongst that number of volunteer rescuers there was one whom I must mention, who, but for the Grace of God would have died on a Scottish road a little over a year before, thanks to a drunken hit-and-run driver. For

Jesse James, one time chairman of the LMRT.   *Aled Taylor*

months Jesse James struggled to survive and eventually recover, with a bagful of screws and plates holding his broken frame together. Yet, on January 2nd, he quietly and unobtrusively joined the searchers. It was a miracle of the first type, that he survived his accident; it is a miracle of the second, that there are people like Jesse whose commitment to helping others in distress transcends the limits of human kindness. Truly the spirit of the Good Samaritan is alive and working today amongst mountain people.

When my dog Gelert fell down that disused mine shaft, and crashed onto the rocks forty feet below, it was a miracle that he survived at all; even more so that his only 'break' was a tooth and that he recovered so quickly, for only five days later he was once again out on an all-night search. It was a miracle, too, that my navigator, Doug Jones, knew the area so well that he was able to find a fifty-metre long disused and flooded tunnel which led into the bottom of the shaft, through which he was able to crawl and bring Gelert to safety.

When news came through to the search base that Robert Hughes and Jillian were safe and well, a great cheer went up from the searchers who had toiled all day and found nothing, for they were all thankful that their combined efforts had ended successfully. Tomorrow, perhaps someone else will be in distress on the mountains. And the Rescue teams and search dog handlers will be ready, yet again, to go out on their next mission.

There's a Time to Call it a Day

The weather forecast was for a rough night on October 2nd 1986, with heavy rain and gale force winds and, when I let the dogs out shortly before 11.00 p.m., the wind was already strengthening and the first drops of rain were spattering on the window panes. The Met office had got it right, and I went to bed thankful that I was not out on the mountain. I switched off the light, turned over and quickly fell asleep. But not for long. In the distance I heard a telephone ringing, though it was in fact right by my bedside. Still half asleep I answered the call, now conscious of the gale driving the rain noisily against the windows. 'God, what a night' I thought as I picked up the receiver.

"Hullo, Bob here," I said. "Evening, Bob," said Harvey Lloyd, my group co-ordinator from Pen-y-Pass, "I hope I haven't got you out of bed. We've got a job on; three medical students from London set off from here at 6.30 p.m. on the last stage of the fourteen peaks, Crib Goch, Carnedd Ugain and Snowdon. They'd arranged to meet their friends in Llanberis at 10.00 p.m. but there's no sign of them at all. Can you get to the police station in Llanberis as soon as possible? Hugh Walton will be there to brief you, and Roland and Phil are also turning out." "O.K. Harvey," I replied, "what about navigators?" "I haven't asked anyone; you know the area so well you don't really need one do you?" "No I suppose not," I said, "but a bit of company would be nice on a night like this. It's filthy weather to have to go out on the hill alone, but never mind."

I got dressed, cursing my luck for having to spend the rest of the night out in the storm, my only company my loyal dog Gelert. But, I reminded myself, anything might have happened to the three missing students. They had been walking all day and had already done eleven of the fourteen peaks and must have been pretty tired when they left Pen-y-Pass. In my opinion it was unwise to attempt the last three peaks along the ridges, heading into a rising gale and torrential rain, knowing that it would be impossible to complete the route in daylight. But it appeared that their determination to finish the course overruled their better judgement.

Down in the warmth of the police station, Hugh Walton briefed the three of us. There was no fresh information and the plan was for Roland to search

Crib Goch ridge from Crib y Ddysgl.   *Tony Welch*

Crib Goch from Pen-y-Pass, Phil was to start at Blaenant, up into Cwm Glas
to Bwlch Goch and then along Crib-y-Ddysgl to Bwlch Glas, and finally I
was to search the Llanberis path to the summit of Snowdon. We expected to
be reasonably close to each other by the time I reached the summit, and we
intended to maintain radio contact with each other as soon as we reached the
ridges. Harvey and Hugh were to remain on listening watch to monitor our
transmissions.

We left the police station at 12.30 a.m. and I drove up to the start of the
Llanberis path at Cader Ellyll. My progress from then on was slow and
uneventful. The weather got steadily worse and by the time I reached the top
of Allt Moses I felt buffeted and almost exhausted. My Goretex weather-
proofs were being put to the most severe test possible, but they kept me
completely dry. I made a radio check call there, but only managed to contact
Harvey at Pen-y-Pass. This did not concern me at this stage as both Phil and

Roland would be shielded by their respective ridges. The time was 2.15 a.m. From then on, as the direction of the path turned straight into the wind, I had to keep my microphone inside my anorak to keep it dry and I was unable to hear any incoming transmissions at all. I had 'battened down all the hatches' to keep out the driving rain and it was all I could do to make any forward progress whatsoever. At times I seemed to be going backwards, but eventually I reached the summit café building at 3.20 a.m. Gelert had by now lost interest and needed a lot of encouragement to leave my side. He was soaked and tired, and clearly not a very happy dog. In any case, with the rain being driven up his nostrils, his scenting ability was minimal.

It happened to be the last night the café staff were staying on the summit before closing for the winter and, although the steel window shutters were already bolted in position, I could see lights burning inside the building. This raised my hopes that perhaps the missing people had made it to the café and had decided to stay there overnight. So for at least ten minutes I banged and shouted all around the building, but my pathetic noise could not compete with the raging storm, and I failed to raise anyone. Disappointed, I gave up the idea and my tiredness and discomfort suddenly seemed much greater, for hopes of a hot drink inside had been dashed! There was no sign of the three students sheltering behind the café, so I moved up to the ridge to get better radio communication, and as soon as I took my microphone out of my anorak I heard Harvey and Hugh discussing my well-being! "Yes, we'd better call out the team", Hugh was saying. "It's an hour and a half since Bob contacted us from Clogwyn station and it's most unlike him not to keep in touch. He must be in some sort of trouble". "I agree" said Harvey, "we won't need many as we know he's somewhere between Clogwyn station and the summit". At this stage I pressed my transmit button and asked for a radio check. "Avalanche 312, this is Peris 70. My location at Glaslyn. You're loud and clear. Where are you?" replied Hugh. "Peris 70, this is Avalanche 312. You're loud and clear. My location on ridge just below the summit. The lights are on in the café, but I cannot get anyone to answer. Possibly the missing people are inside. Otherwise nothing seen or heard. Conditions up here are diabolical and I want to come down". "O.K., Bob. I'm at the outflow of Glaslyn. Make your way down here. You may meet Roland who is making his way up towards The Zigzags". "Peris 70, Avalanche 312, Roger. See you soon." It was very encouraging to know that down below my colleagues were monitoring our progress high up in the storm, and that they were on the point of calling out a team to start looking for me. I recalled a period of static warfare during the Korean war when I made a rule that I would never leave my radio and turn in, until all my patrols were safely back inside the company perimeter. The knowledge that the company commander was ready to act if a patrol should run into trouble did a lot to maintain morale, and I had now experienced the same thing myself.

With the storm temporarily at our backs, Gelert and I walked down to Bwlch Glas and found the monolith marking the start of The Zigzag descent to Glaslyn. Water was pouring off the slopes on to the path and it was like walking down a river. After feeling my way for about two hundred metres, at a point where the path goes through a rocky area I became completely disorientated. The shadows thrown by my lamp were distorted by the mist and sheets of driven rain, and I could not recognise any features on a path which in daylight I must have walked hundreds of times. I was walking blind and was almost certain I had gone off the path and was heading into danger. So I walked back to the monolith to reassure myself that I was on the right path. I was right, and once again started down. I knew I was tired and my mind was not reacting as sharply as it should, but this time I forced myself to concentrate, and slowly but surely I worked across the rocky area which included a rock step and a narrow ledge, until I was on to a wider and easier path. But it still required great care.

Near the intersection of the Pyg and Miners Tracks, I met Roland. He told me that both he and Phil had decided that conditions were so bad it would have been suicidal to attempt to traverse either Crib Goch or Crib-y-Ddysgl ridges, and that Phil had searched Cwm Glas and parts of North Ridge, and he had searched as far up the east ridge of Crib Goch as he could, compatible with safety, before returning to Bwlch Moch and working up the Pyg Track. He was now intending to continue up to Bwlch Glas, try to reach the Pinnacles on the south-west side of Carnedd Ugain, and then to rejoin Hugh and me down at Glaslyn.

Roland and Phil had made the wise decision. It would have been crazy to go on the exposed ridges in that gale, as both they and their dogs would have found it very difficult to stand up, let alone walk safely along them. It has always been a sound philosophy in MR that the rescuers must avoid becoming the rescued. My route up the Llanberis path was bad enough, especially from Clogwyn station onwards, but nowhere was I exposed to the full force of the storm on a narrow ridge as Roland and Phil would have been, and I was never at the same degree of risk.

I left Roland and made my way slowly down to Glaslyn where I joined Hugh. "My Land-rover is at the crushing mill" he said. "I'll just tell Roland that we'll wait for him there. No point in staying out in this rain; we might as

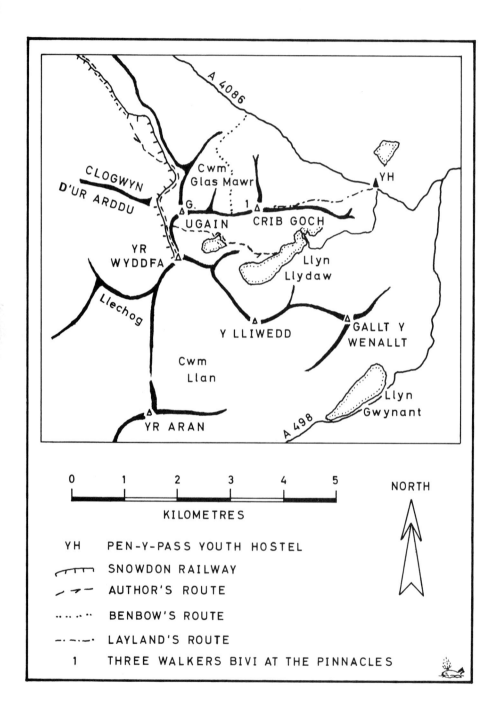

CLOGWYN
D'UR ARDDU

Cwm
Glas Mawr

Y

YH

G.
UGAIN

1
CRIB GOCH

YR
WYDDFA

Llyn
Llydaw

Llechog

Y LLIWEDD

GALLT Y
WENALLT

Cwm
Llan

Llyn
Gwynant

YR ARAN

A 498

| 0 | 1 | 2 | 3 | 4 | 5 |

KILOMETRES

NORTH

YH   PEN-Y-PASS YOUTH HOSTEL

　　　 SNOWDON RAILWAY

　　　 AUTHOR'S ROUTE

　　　 BENBOW'S ROUTE

　　　 LAYLAND'S ROUTE

1   THREE WALKERS BIVI AT THE PINNACLES

well get what shelter we can in the vehicle". This done, Roland acknowledged the message and said he was already on his way down The Zigzags. So we would not have long to wait. It was now 4.30 a.m. and as soon as Roland joined us we drove to Pen-y-Pass Youth Hostel where Harvey was waiting for us in the kitchen. A hot drink and one of their famous flapjacks put new life into us. There was still no news of the missing students, and we thought it likely that they had run into some difficulty somewhere along the ridges. The storm had eased off, and Hugh decided to call out the Llanberis team for first light.

At 9.00 a.m. a party doing a line search from Cader Ellyll towards the summit of Snowdon, and as far as possible covering both the Llanberis path and the railway line, met the three students striding happily down to Llanberis. They were blissfully unaware of the events during the night, and of the concern for their safety, caused by their failure to turn up in Llanberis as planned. They explained that they had reached the western end of Crib Goch ridge just before dark and, in view of the worsening conditions, they realised it would be irresponsible to try to complete their route. They could either drop down the scree on to the Pyg Track and return to Pen-y-Pass, or they could shelter as best they could in the Pinnacles at the end of the ridge. If they had done the first, they would have failed to complete the fourteen peaks, so they opted for the second. In fact they were quite safe and in no real danger, although they spent a cold, sleepless and uncomfortable night crouching amongst the rocks. But we were not to know that, and one can hardly blame them for their final decision to stay put. Their mistake was to press on from Pen-y-Pass so late in the day, more so as they had been told about the forecast of the approaching storm. Prudent and responsible mountaineers know when it's time to call it a day and abort the expedition. It's not cowardly to turn back when the situation demands it; it's the sensible thing to do, and after all there is always another day. Everyone concerned was relieved when the three young people walked off the mountain, safe and well, but it would have been nice to get a letter of thanks, would it not?

Heroes of the Glass Mountain

Well, that was the headline in the Daily Mail on Monday February 5th 1979.

Winter in Snowdonia is very much an unknown quantity. Sometimes there is snow on the high tops as early as October, only to disappear again within a few days, and you can be fairly certain that any snow falling before Christmas will be short-lived. From then onwards it is normal for there to be some lying snow until April, but occasionally the mountain railway cuttings are blocked as late as the end of May. Conditions during the period from Christmas 1978 until Easter 1979 were some of the most severe in living memory. Heavy snowfall and freezing air temperatures resulted in huge frozen drifts all over the mountains, and you could walk on to the roof of the summit building from the far end of the station platform! From mid-January until Easter, Snowdon was covered in deep, frozen snow and ice, and was truly a 'glass mountain'. It is not surprising that the rescue services were kept very busy during this time and it is interesting to note that the last pocket of snow, on the north face of Lliwedd, was still just visible on July 10th. To underline the severity of the conditions – just before Easter, Steve Mitchell, the secretary of the Llanberis MRT (a very experienced mountaineer, British Mountain Guide and one-time instructor for 5½ years at the Scottish National Mountain Centre) issued a warning statement that . . . 'high mountain paths are deeply covered in snow and ice, and almost all should be considered grade 1 snow and ice climbs on which experienced mountaineers use ice-axes, crampons and ropes. This, together with very difficult navigation, sometimes in white-out conditions, means that even experts are needing to use all their skills . . . ' He added that, notwithstanding this, he fully defended the rights of individuals to go into the mountains, but the message was a timely warning to all, especially those lacking experience.

On Saturday February 3rd there was snow above 300 metres with a complete white-out above 800 metres. At about 10.00 a.m. 45-year-old Clive Cartwright and his friend James Watkinson, 36, parked their car at Pont Bethania at the bottom of the Watkin Path in Nant Gwynant and set out to climb to the summit of Snowdon. It was extremely cold with heavily-iced

66

deep snow high up and, as they approached the summit along Bwlch-y-Saethau, mist came down creating a near white-out. This caused them to veer slightly away from the path and they made an involuntary steep ascent to the summit which they reached at 4.00 p.m. *En route* they had been seen by Brian Pemberton, who noticed that only one of them had an ice-axe and the other was not well equipped for such an expedition in 'arctic conditions'. Neither of the men had crampons and no ropes were in evidence.

In the course of my research into this incident, I was in correspondence with Jim Watkinson, and I can do no better than to quote his own moving account of the whole tragic weekend: ' . . . Although Clive Cartwright had been on Snowdon many times before, this was my first experience of the mountains and was my first trip out with him. I had known Clive for about two years; he was a good character and I enjoyed his company. He had invited me to join him for a weekend walking in Snowdonia and he explained that along with other friends and colleagues they made a bi-annual ascent of Snowdon each year (once in February and again in August). I was happy to accept the invitation as I enjoy the outdoors and countryside, and we set off for Snowdonia on February 2nd, arriving in time to make an ascent of Moel Siabod before dark. The weather was very good throughout this day with clear blue skies and warm sunshine. The landscape was beautiful with lots of very deep snow and of course hard icy surfaces as well.

I was wearing a couple of pullovers and a pair of trousers over a track suit. My footwear consisted of football socks and a pair of industrial working boots, and I also had a lightweight nylon anorak and a pair of leather gloves. Clive wore a couple of pullovers, a pair of lightweight trousers, socks and a pair of walking boots. We had one ice-axe and a compass between us and I now well know that we were totally ill-equipped for the Alpine conditions which we were to encounter.

The two of us set off together on the Saturday morning to climb Snowdon via the Watkin Path. Eventually we reached the cloud line and soon became disorientated. The thought did occur to me that conditions were somewhat risky, but foolishly we carried on. At about 3.00 p.m., whilst negotiating a steep ascent on icy surfaces, Clive suggested that we might not reach the summit and that perhaps we should go back. However, he said 'Let's give it one more try.' I remember seeing several other climbers passing us at this stage as we were resting. They were equipped with ice-axes, ropes, helmets, crampons etc.

We carried on upwards, Clive leading, and I followed, using steps he had cut with his ice-axe. It was an extremely dodgy situation, but we finally reached the top and after a short break and a bite to eat we began the descent via the mountain railway which was completely covered by deep ice and snow. At this time it began snowing and the wind became quite strong. Visibility was no more than 3 to 4 metres and once again we became disorientated and were not at all certain of our direction. At the time I suggested to Clive that maybe we should return to the summit and make shelter for the night (it was probably after 4.00 p.m. by this time).

We carried on, attempting to follow a compass bearing (north-westerly, I think), but Clive, who wore glasses, said that they were icing up and he couldn't see the compass very well. He passed the compass to me to attempt to follow, but soon after that my feet slipped from under me and I began to slide down on my backside. I tried digging in with the heels of my boots and knuckles on my hands in a vain effort to brake my slide, but I was picking up speed all the time. I hit a rock feet first, and this spun me round so that now I was sliding down on my back, head first, and shot into space. I thought that this was the end for me and I had visions of my head being smashed to pieces, thinking what a stupid mess we had got ourselves into.

I remember the impact as I hit the ground again which knocked me out completely. Then I recall regaining consciousness and I was face down on my chest, spitting snow from my mouth. As I picked myself up I couldn't believe that I was still alive. I looked around me and realised that I had fallen way below the cloud line. I could see a small frozen lake below me but up above all I could see was cloud and mountain ridges and I seemed to be enclosed in a large basin. I tried shouting up to Clive, but couldn't make contact; I couldn't hear anything and it was all very quiet. I never made contact with, or saw, Clive again.

I decided that the only thing I could do was to continue as best I could on my own, as I was still in the ice, snow, and sub-zero temperatures, and it would soon be dark. With several injuries which included a strained back and ankle, badly bruised hip, wrenched shoulder and numerous cuts and bruises, I staggered on and after reaching the top of the nearest ridge I began making my way downwards. It had now become dark, and I had not the slightest idea where I was, so I sheltered in bits of bushes and grass tussocks by a stream, and put on a heavy, bright orange anorak which Clive had lent me.

During the night I twice saw the rescue helicopter, but my torch (a bicycle lamp which was in my rucksack) had been damaged in the fall, so I was unable to make any kind of signal. Soon after daybreak I made very little progress; I was so sore with the cold and bruising that I could hardly move.

'The Glass Mountain': Snow-covered Crib Goch (right) and Snowdon.   John Roberts

The rest I think you know. I almost cried when the RAF lads came across from the helicopter to help me.

I will never forget this incident and the efforts made by the various rescue parties. Clive loved the mountains; in fact, the day before we climbed Snowdon he told me that if he were to die, he would like it to be in Snowdonia. In the event, at his request made in his Will, we scattered his ashes from the summit of Snowdon during the summer of 1979.'

The place where Jim Watkinson slipped over the edge is fully described in chapter 26, 'Clogwyn Goch – The Killer Convex'.

During the early part of the evening of Saturday, some of Cartwright's and Watkinson's friends were waiting for them as previously arranged in the Pen-y-Gwryd Hotel, and as time went on and the pair did not show up, concern was felt for their safety. Their car at Pont Bethania was checked out and, a search of the roads around the Snowdon massif proving negative, at 9.45 p.m. the police were informed. The Snowdonia National Park Head Warden and leader of the Llanberis MRT, John Ellis Roberts, was alerted and what turned out to be an extensive search operation began.

At about the time that James Watkinson fell during the afternoon, two climbers who had set out to climb on Clogwyn-y-Garnedd on the east face of Snowdon completed their climb and they too set off to walk on compass bearings down the Llanberis path. By about 9.00 p.m. they had not arrived back at their base and were also reported missing, so that the search operation was for two separate couples, although they were known to be in roughly the same area. Soon after 10.00 p.m. on Saturday night, the cloud began to lift and before midnight the summit was clear and bathed in the light of a full moon. It was thought worthwhile to ask 22 Squadron, SAR helicopters, to overfly the area using the under-fuselage searchlight, and see if they could pick up any tracks in the bright moonlight. Accompanied by two members of the Llanberis MRT, John Ellis Roberts and John Jackson, the helicopter crew was able to identify a number of footprints but they all petered out on the hard, frozen ground around the summit, and the search was abandoned at 2.00 a.m. The temperature recorded at RAF Valley fell to $-3°C$ in the Snowdon area during the night.

At 7.00 a.m. next morning, Sunday February 4th, a helicopter air-lifted members of the team and five SARDA dog teams to various points around Snowdon, whilst other groups started to search lower down, working

John Jackson.   *John B. Jackson colln.*

John Ellis Roberts   *John B. Jackson colln.*

upwards along the main routes to the summit. While this was being done, a second helicopter took John Ellis Roberts on an aerial search and achieved two quick successes. The first was when a 47-year-old climber, who had made himself a snowhole after losing contact with his companion in the white-out, was found close to Clogwyn station. He was suffering from hypothermia and was airlifted to base for treatment and questioning. The aerial search then continued along and below the railway line, and through Cwm d'ur Arddu. Immediately below Clogwyn Goch what appeared to be a trail of blood and footmarks were seen leading downhill in the direction of 'Halfway House' brew shack on the Llanberis path. Soon after starting to follow this trail, John spotted a man propped against the wall of an old sheep shelter waving weakly to the helicopter. He was James Watkinson, who had survived a fall of 250 metres, bouncing and sliding from one pocket of snow to another, miraculously missing the jagged crags as he fell. In spite of the injuries he had sustained as described in his own story, he had managed to stagger about half a mile to near the sheep pen, where he got what shelter he could throughout the bitterly cold night. He was the second of the four missing men to be found and he, too, was airlifted to Bangor hosital.

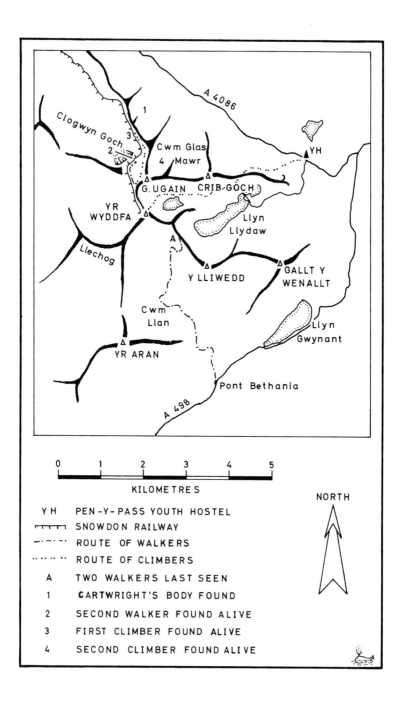

KILOMETRES

NORTH

YH   PEN-Y-PASS YOUTH HOSTEL

    SNOWDON RAILWAY

    ROUTE OF WALKERS

    ROUTE OF CLIMBERS

A   TWO WALKERS LAST SEEN

1   CARTWRIGHT'S BODY FOUND

2   SECOND WALKER FOUND ALIVE

3   FIRST CLIMBER FOUND ALIVE

4   SECOND CLIMBER FOUND ALIVE

In the meantime the search parties and dog teams were systematically covering the whole of Snowdon, from the summit northwards over Carnedd Ugain and down into Cwm Glas, and on the south side across to Lliwedd and down South Ridge into Cwm Tregalan and Cwm-y-Llan. The party I was with included Chris Wharmby and his two dogs, and three other team members. This was one of the last occasions in which SARDA (Wales) was involved when handlers were allowed to work more than one dog at a time. We were flown round to the north end of Bwlch-y-Saethau, where the helicopter hovered about 2 metres above the ground while we jumped out on to the ridge. Having been literally 'dropped off', we waited for the winchman to drop our rucksacks on to the flattest place we could find. Unfortunately his aim with the last one, which belonged to Cyril Jones, my partner for this search, was just off the mark and the sack slid off the ridge, ending up 250 metres below on frozen Glaslyn. The helicopter went down and was able to recover the rucksack but Cyril's ice-axe and crampons, which had been strapped to it, had been torn away and were lying somewhere on the precipitous slope. We were now faced with a difficult and dangerous traverse across the snow slopes above Cwm Tregalan, which was our search area, and in the interests of safety we made a slow and careful descent along Bwlch-y-Saethau to Bwlch Ciliau, thence down into Cwm Tregalan taking long zigzags across the less steep slopes. The going got easier as we descended, but it still needed care.

The dogs were also having considerable difficulty in getting across the top slopes under South Ridge, and as we made our first traverse back from Bwlch Ciliau, we saw one of Chris's dogs lose his foothold and take a long slide until he managed to stop himself in some softer snow. He rejoined Chris further along the ridge, none the worse for his mishap.

The second of the two climbers, aged thirty-two, was found at mid-morning some 330 metres down the slope of Gyrn Las into Cwm Glas. His companion, the first to be found and rescued, had been able to pinpoint the spot where they had become separated, and one of the search parties had been directed to that area. The man was unconscious and was flown to hospital suffering from severe head injuries. Sadly, he never recovered consciousness and he died seven and a half months later. At the inquest the survivor told the coroner that they were taking the route of the Llanberis path on compass bearings, probing the snow ahead of them with their ice-axes. At one point they stopped on the edge of a cliff, took five paces back and took a new bearing. After six more paces his companion disappeared.

The last of the four to be accounted for was found by Steve Mitchell and his party after two walkers, whom they had met above Cwm Glas, told him they had seen an ice-axe and balaclava just below the ridge on the Cwm Glas Bach side. Steve and his group made a 100 metre diagonal descent of the cliff face and found Clive Cartwright's body lying in the snow. He had extensive back and head injuries and a serious fracture of the right femur. He had no detectable pulse and, in view of the nature and severity of his injuries, it was obvious he had been dead for a considerable time. He was evacuated by helicopter.

There are some interesting points to consider about this incident, both cause and effect, but the predominant impression I had at the time was the invaluable part played by the helicopters. Without their help, to have achieved what they did would have taken ground searchers – without the advantage of a bird's-eye view – very much longer in the most risky and dangerous conditions many of those taking part had ever experienced. Having been an Infantry officer for many years, it was natural for me to compare the way search and rescue operations were carried out with Army practices, and on this occasion I wrote in my diary that, 'the whole operation was well thought out. Deployment of ground searchers and dog teams was excellent, no part of the mountain was left uncovered, and the best use seemed to have been made of the resources available to John Roberts.' The only problem, I thought, was radio communication, for with search parties scattered all round the summit the only certain way communications could have worked efficiently would have been either by establishing a control station on the summit itself, or by setting up a series of link stations round the base of the mountain. Neither of these options was feasible, and the only way was to rely on search parties relaying messages one to the other or to base. In general this worked quite well, but down in Cwm Tregalan we soon lost contact with everyone else until we reached Pont Bethania, where we received the 'stop' message.

Incidents happen for a variety of reasons and probably nearly all are avoidable. In the case of Cartwright and Watkinson, it seems that Cartwright frequently walked up Snowdon, but Watkinson said that this was his first experience of the mountains. There was no evidence, however, that Cartwright had experienced snow and ice conditions, certainly not of the severity with which they had to contend on this fateful day. The evidence shows that they were hopelessly ill-equipped to face the hazards high up, and they should never have pressed on into the white-out above cloud base. Even when, in Jim Watkinson's own story, he tells of serious doubts in both their minds about the wisdom of going on, they did so. It was an over-ambitious expedition which, not surprisingly, ended in disaster.

The two climbers, however, were fully and properly equipped with crampons, axes and helmets, and were roped for the actual climb. What actually happened is best described by what was said at the inquest. The survivor told the coroner that during the climb on Carned-y-Garnedd the weather deteriorated and that, when they reached the ridge just below the summit of Snowdon, they found themselves in a white-out and could not see even their own feet. They decided to follow the tourists' path down to Llanberis on compass bearings, but something went seriously wrong with their navigation. Those who have never been in a white-out can have no idea how frightening it can be. You have no horizon and to move at all is like walking in pitch darkness – completely blind and disorientated. Whether or not the two climbers had prepared for the conditions in which they found themselves will never be known. However, with the benefit of hindsight, the one lesson which must be learned from this incident is that if there is the slightest possibility (and there **always** is) of conditions being so bad that compass bearings will be needed, the route to safety should be worked out carefully and accurately in warmth and comfort **before** setting out. It is too late when you are in a freezing white-out or a force eight gale, for no one can work out a route, especially on an exposed ridge, with sufficient accuracy in wind, rain or snow, often made worse by fatigue.

The point where the climber disapeared over the edge into Cwm Glas was at least 100 metres from the Llanberis path at its nearest point, and only 1,000 metres from the starting point at the top of their climb. In a straight line this represents an error of six degrees, and whether the mistake was made in working out the bearings or in actually walking on them is immaterial. Either way, such an error can easily lead to disaster – as it did in this case. To be able to navigate accurately in bad weather requires a great deal of practice, not only in working out a route, but also in walking it, but occasionally conditions can defeat even the most competent of navigators as appears to have happened here. Dead reckoning is a skill which is seldom required by climbers as opposed to walkers, but it must be one which it is worth learning in case of need. It is a matter of regret that more hill-walkers do not pay sufficient attention to it for, as I learned as a young officer cadet, 'time spent in reconnaissance is never wasted'. The same rule certainly applies here – but for 'reconnaissance' substitute 'preparation'.

Point of No Return

April 1979, Easter Week, and there was still deep snow above 600 metres. The weather was far from settled and the forecasters predicted continuing arctic conditions for some time to come. Warnings were put out by the police and warden service, and even the local coroner had announced that his mortuary was 'ready for foolish Easter climbers who venture unwisely or ill-equipped on Snowdonia peaks'. On Thursday April 12th the forecast was for a rapid deterioration, with wind speed increasing to storm force from the south-west accompanied by sleet and snow. It was timed for midday onwards, and proved to be entirely accurate.

At about 10.00 a.m. Mr John Mountain, a forty-four-year-old consultant surgeon from Essex who was an experienced mountain walker, set out with his twelve-year-old daughter Alison, intending to walk as far as practicable across Crib Goch and Crib-y-Ddysgl ridges to the summit of Snowdon. They both had ice-axes, but no crampons, and carried in their rucksacks sufficient food and spare warm clothing. But it seems that they were unaware of the severe weather warnings.

Mr Mountain had apparently promised Alison that he would take her over the ridges during the Easter holidays, but it was said that he had only recently recovered from an attack of flu, and if that was true there would be a danger of quickly running out of energy. The debilitating effects of flu would have meant that energy levels had not been sufficiently restored to undertake such an expedition, certainly not in the prevailing arctic conditions.

As they made their way on to Crib Goch the wind was already beginning to strengthen, but the weather was still fair. It was then that Roderick Malcolm Campbell, who was doing the same route on his own, caught up with them and, having reached the summit of Crib Goch at about 1.15 p.m., they decided to walk together and carry on to Carnedd Ugain, the summit at the western end of Crib-y-Ddysgl. By the time they were ascending that ridge, the wind was blowing at gale force with rain and sleet and, worse still, they were walking directly into it, which is a most exhausting process at any time. They took a short rest, during which they took stock of the situation and decided that they had reached the point of no return. The best option appeared to be to press on rather than turn back and have to face the somewhat 'dicy' traverse of Crib Goch and descent of the East ridge in such violent winds. But by the time they reached the summit of Carnedd Ugain, John Mountain had started to show signs of tiredness and exposure, and progress became slower. The weather conditions continued to worsen, a blizzard developed and visibility became very poor. Alison, too, was tiring by now but was able to continue with occasional rests and they made a decision to drop down to the railway line and follow the track down towards Llanberis. After almost a mile John Mountain was showing increasing signs of hypothermia, his condition was deteriorating fast and he could hardly go on. In spite of all the encouragement and support both Alison and Roderick Campbell could give him, by the time they got across Clogwyn Goch he could go no further. He kept falling in the snow, his movements were uncoordinated and he had difficulty in speaking. It was now 5.15 p.m. and Roderick realised that it was going to be impossible to get the surgeon off the hill, as he was completely exhausted and mentally confused. As there was no one else about, he decided to dig a snow hole and get John Mountain and Alison into it. Helped by Alison he dug a hole about a metre deep into which they had to get Mr Mountain inside a polythene bag, and Alison then got into the bag with him. She, too, was very tired by this time and Roderick was

Crib Goch, Crib y Ddysgl and Carnedd Ugain – the point of no return   *Tony Welch*

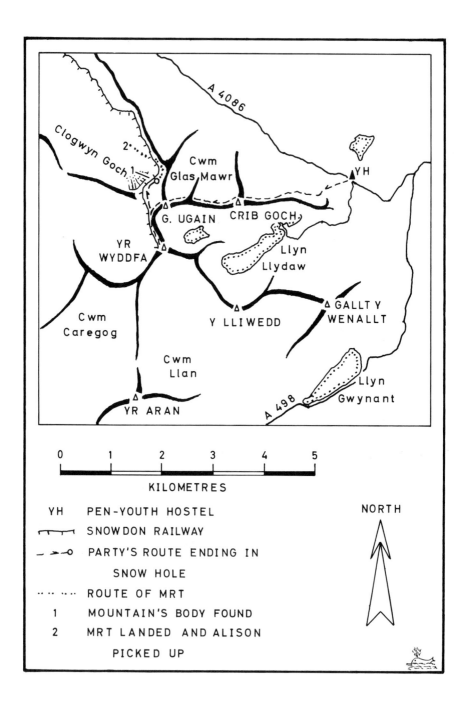

KILOMETRES

0 1 2 3 4 5

YH   PEN-YOUTH HOSTEL

SNOWDON RAILWAY

PARTY'S ROUTE ENDING IN

SNOW HOLE

ROUTE OF MRT

1   MOUNTAIN'S BODY FOUND

2   MRT LANDED AND ALISON

PICKED UP

NORTH

becoming concerned for her as well. Both of them felt very cold, but they would be warmer in the snow-hole than outside, exposed to the gale and snow. He gave them what food he had and impressed on them that he was going down to Llanberis for help, and that they must stay in the hole until help arrived.

It took Roderick far longer than usual to reach the village as he was walking straight into the storm and it was growing dusk when, at 7.30 p.m., he reported what had happened to the Llanberis police. Immediately a full scale call-out was put into operation and, in spite of the atrocious weather, a helicopter from Valley was scrambled to land at the Llanberis MRT base in Nant Peris. I had originally been called out to rendezvous at Pen-y-Pass and that is where I met Roderick Campbell being interviewed by a police officer. He told me his story, and then I went down to Nant Peris where the team was already assembling.

It was after 8.00 p.m. when I arrived at base, and the helicopter was just taking off with the first party of MRT personnel, led by Hugh Walton and Steve Mitchell. I was asked to go round to Hafodty Newydd and set up a radio link there between base and the incident site which was in direct line of sight, and I prepared for a long, busy and cold night in a vehicle constantly buffeted and shaken by the storm. Soon after I arrived at Hafodty, the helicopter attempted to land the second lift of MRT members from Nant Peris. He had experienced considerable difficulty in landing the first party on the flat ground at the bottom of Allt Moses, and I watched him making repeated efforts to get down with the second group. But the storm had become even fiercer in the meantime, and the pilot decided to give it best and return his load to base. This group was then brought round to my position at Hafodty by road.

After establishing radio contact with the first group, they set off to join up with them on the railway line above Clogwyn station. Rather than waste any more time, Hugh Walton and his party set off to try to find the snow-hole, and were soon struggling against the severe blizzard in deep snow, to the east of the station. As they pressed on up the railway line they were frequently unable to stand up in the gusts which were estimated to be up to ninety mph. At one time a particularly strong gust took hold of the stretcher and dragged the four men holding it for several metres. Progress was very slow, the team members often crawling on their hands and knees.

At about 9.30 p.m. Hugh Walton almost fell into the snow-hole, which was only a metre and a half from the edge of a steep scree slope at the lower end of Clogwyn Goch. A small voice greeted him, "Oh hullo, have you come

Left to right: Snowdon, Crib Goch and Carnedd Ugain seen across Cwm Ffynnon from the Miners Track on the Glyders.   *Author*

to rescue me?" and the search for Alison was over. The little girl was in surprisingly good shape considering her ordeal and she was able to tell her rescuers that her father had become increasingly confused and "had not been talking sensibly." He "was not himself at all" and he had said "we'll have to try to go from here." In spite of Alison's entreaties and efforts to keep him in the comparative warmth of the snow hole, he had eventually got out of the polythene bag some time after dark, saying that he was too hot. Alison had done all she could to save her father, but the effects of hypothermia had so confused him that he was no longer able to reason properly. There was now no sign of John Mountain and in view of what Alison had told the rescue party it was obvious that he was suffering from advanced hypothermia. As every member of the team up there was needed to stretcher Alison safely down to the roadhead at Hafodty where I was situated, no further search was made for him that night in view of the extremely dangerous conditions and the serious risks involved.

By the time the stretcher party had reached the bottom of Allt Moses, the storm had eased off a bit and the helicopter pilot, who had been standing-by at Nant Peris in case he could be of further assistance, said he would try to pick Alison up and fly her to hospital in Bangor. Their wait had been worthwhile, and without any great difficulty they soon had Alison on board and *en route* for hospital whilst the exhausted MRT men made their way down to my position at Hafodty Newydd where I had laid on transport to ferry them back to base.

It now remained to find John Mountain himself, but we all knew deep down when Alison was found alone in the snow hole that there was very little hope of finding him alive. Hypothermia is a quick killer, but next morning we went out still hoping that a miracle might have happened and that we were going to find him alive. More dog teams were called out and were deployed to work the area along and below the railway line, in Cwm d'ur Arddu and on Gyrn Las. The rest of the available Llanberis MRT members and the RAF MRT from Valley also joined the search.

I was with three others to be airlifted into Cwm Glas – John Jackson, Cyril Jones and my nineteen-year-old son Jonathan – but the helicopter had a problem in getting above the lip of the hanging cwm in the face of the still gusting wind, and we had to jump out on to a slope covered with frozen snow and ice – a most daunting operation which brought me nearer to refusing to obey an order than throughout my whole life! But pride prevailed and we all managed to land safely and start our search of Cwm Glas. It was a few minutes after 9.30 a.m. when we heard the recall message on my radio.

John Mountain's body had been found and recovered from the rocks some 175 metres below the railway line. His spectacles and gold watch had been found near the snow-hole, on the edge of the cutting from where he had fallen, and he had suffered severe head and other injuries.

There was much speculation about the cause and effect of this unhappy incident. Had he left the snow-hole because he thought he could get help, or was he in the late stages of hypothermia and, as he said to Alison, thinking that he was too hot. All the evidence points to the fact that he had become progressively more disorientated, which is a typical symptom of hypothermia. Alison herself survived the ordeal and was well enough to be discharged from hospital next day.

Snowdon Horror Plunge

This was a typical, and unusually accurate, headline about a particularly nasty incident which occurred a few days before Christmas, 1984. There was a coating of snow and ice over the upper reaches of the footpaths to the summit of Snowdon, which was a trap for the unwary.

At around 5.00 p.m. I received a phone call telling me that a girl student had fallen from the Watkin Path and had disappeared into Cwm Tregalan, 300 metres or more below. One of the party of four, who had also fallen about 150 metres, had managed to struggle down to raise the alarm leaving the other two young men to try to locate the girl, and then make their way down to the road in Nant Gwynant. I made all speed round to Pont Bethania where I met up with two other members of the team, who also happened to be dog handlers. Our philosophy is that while there is no proof of death, there is hope, regardless of what an informant may say. It is our job to go out and find the casualty in the hope that we might still be in time. We treat every search as an emergency, and so it was in this case.

We met the two informants by the phone box and got as much detail from them as we could. But both were suffering from shock and were very emotional, and quite unable to give us an accurate fix of the girl's location. They described how they had found the casualty slightly head-down, wedged between two rocks where she had come to rest at the end of her fall. She was unconscious, and had a severe laceration to her scalp which had bled profusely, and the shiny covering of the skull was exposed. Neither of the young men had an adequate knowledge of first-aid, and they assumed, quite wrongly, that this was her brain and that she must be dead. As it happened, the position she was in was ideal for an unconscious person, as she was firmly held by the two rocks and could not have slipped any further, and any fluid matter would have drained away out of her mouth and not down her windpipe into her lungs. It was a perfect 'recovery' position, adapted to a rocky environment, but, as a last pathetic gesture, her distraught friends propped her up in a sitting position to 'make her look more comfortable'. This information really did set the adrenalin rushing, and we set about starting the search with tremendous urgency.

Cwm Tregalan and Bwlch y Saethau seen from the slopes of Yr Aran.   *John Roberts*

Heather Maling and Phil Benbow were the other two handlers, and we decided to get them up into the search area immediately, as there must be a chance that the girl was still alive. It was just dark by now, and a helicopter from 22 Squadron was fast approaching from Valley to see if he could help.

I called him up and asked him to land to take the two dog teams on board and fly them as high up the cwm as possible. The pilot acknowledged, but he had a problem finding a suitable landing pad and asked if he could land on the road by the bridge. I switched on my red-and-white flashing roof-light, and the traffic police, who had arrived and were standing by, went into action and stopped the traffic while the helicopter came in, picked up the dog teams, and lifted them into Cwm Tregalan.

The road was not closed for more than a few minutes, but the irritation it caused to one or two furious drivers on their way home from work was unbelievable. Even when the reason was explained, their attitude was that 'they' should not have been fooling about on the mountains in these conditions. It is always 'in these conditions', when those who do not understand why people enjoy walking or climbing have to voice their criticism, but more about this elsewhere in the book.

I had a link radio in my car and was able to establish communications with the rescue base at Pen-y-Pass, and was also well-placed to maintain good communications with dog teams and rescue parties who would be on a straight line-of-sight through Cwm-y-Llan into Cwm Tregalan.

Hugh Walton, the Llanberis MRT leader, arrived with six team members soon after the helicopter had disappeared into the mountains, and I brought him up to date about the search already being put in hand by the two dog teams. Some of the rescue team with first-aid equipment and a stretcher made their way up the Watkin Path, whilst another ten men, who arrived a little later, were airlifted in by the helicopter, which had to make two more landings on the road. Heather and Phil reported back that ground conditions up there were very difficult and that it was particularly dangerous negotiating the steep, icy slopes in the dark. Even the dogs were slithering and sliding as they quartered the ground. Whilst the dogs were working high up the Cwm, Hugh deployed his men lower down, their job being to traverse across the slopes and gradually work their way up towards Phil and Heather. In this way their scents would not distract and confuse the dogs.

Having dropped the last group of team members, the helicopter tried to overfly the area using his 'underbelly' searchlight. But the weather had become a lot worse, the wind had increased, snow had begun to fall, and their efforts were pointless. One of the crew commented later "It was pretty rough up there." Quite an under-statement!

The ground-searchers were finding the going more and more exhausting and it had become a slow and increasingly dangerous operation. Just after 11.30 p.m. Phil's dog, Jet, followed a tenuous scent across a snow-filled gully and over a small ridge to find the girl. The team members now closed in, but it was too late; she was already dead and rigor mortis had set in. All they could do was to stretcher her body down to the road, as the helicopter had long since gone back to base. The team started to make the journey through Cwm Tregalan, but some members were almost exhausted and it was imperative to get them off the mountain as soon as possible before hypothermia set in. The attempt to recover the girl's body was abandoned until daylight when the helicopter airlifted her to hospital in Bangor.

In an incident such as this, when the approximate location of the casualty is known and there is no information about his condition, it must be assumed that he is still alive and that by prompt action he can be rescued and his life saved. This is the real crisis and requires immediate action. In this incident, as soon as we had spoken to the informants, not a moment was wasted in getting the search dog teams into action and we were lucky that the helicopter arrived on the scene at the critical moment. At least an hour of precious time was saved by airlifting the dog teams into the search area. However, the decision to abandon the attempt to bring the girl's body down until daylight came in for some criticism which we all felt was unjustified. Whilst it is accepted that only a doctor can certify that a casualty is actually dead, experienced rescue personnel know beyond reasonable doubt when death has occurred, especially if rigor mortis has set in. Normally a rescue team will complete the recovery of a deceased casualty in one operation, and in fact this was the only occasion I can remember when we left a body out on the hill overnight and unattended.

The law of the land lays down very strict rules of procedure when dealing with a death, more so when it has occurred by violent external means such as a fall down a mountainside. But these were exceptional circumstances. A team leader is responsible for the safety and well-being of his members and there may come a time when he has to decide to call off a search, or indeed a rescue operation, if in his opinion continuing is likely to result in team members becoming casualties. The weather had become so vile that some of the rescue team were already showing early signs of hypothermia and expressed concern about their own condition to Hugh. His responsibility then was to get his team safely down to the road and, since he had no possible doubts that the girl was dead, he made the decision to leave her on the hill and seek refuge in the valley. Before the party left her, they made her completely secure, and treated her with the utmost deference. The police and medical authorities made their point, but it was accepted that in the circumstances Hugh Walton had no option and had made the correct decision.

Double Incident

January and February 1985 produced what the police described as 'a never-ending catalogue of accidents'. The mountains of Snowdonia were covered with deep snow and ice and a bitterly cold, sub-zero easterly wind, blowing straight across the North European plain from Siberia, had set in and lasted for several weeks, often producing an extremely severe wind-chill effect. During the first four months of 1985 there was a high incident rate for all MRTs in Snowdonia, most of the accidents being due to slips or falls in the iced-up conditions.

On the afternoon of Sunday February 10th the freezing east wind was blowing at gale force even at low levels. I had taken my dogs for a walk but turned back when I could make no headway against the wind, and I had just got home when the phone rang. It was Harvey Lloyd at Pen-y-Pass, asking me to get up there as soon as possible as there were two separate incidents on Snowdon. I could not believe it and said "Stop fooling around, Harvey. No-one could be mad enough to be out on the hill in this weather". But he assured me he was not fooling around, and within twenty-five minutes I was in Pen-y-Pass carpark discussing the situation with Harvey and Phil Benbow. They were ready to move off up the Pyg Track to deal with the nearer of the two incidents, and Harvey asked me to take over rescue control, which meant a long and busy night, but I would be inside and reasonably comfortable. He gave me a quick briefing and told me that the RAF Valley MRT were in the Bethesda area and that the police had been asked to contact them and get them round to Pen-y-Pass as soon as possible. A few members of the Llanberis team had already been called out and Harvey suggested that I should call everyone on the call-out list as the two incidents were widely separated and we would need a large number of people.

The nearer of the two incidents had been reported by a fourteen-year-old boy whose father had fallen 10 metres on the rock band on the east ridge of Crib Goch. The boy's twin brother also appeared to have fallen but was relatively unhurt and had stayed with the father who had chest pains and was finding it difficult to breathe. Harvey and Phil set off to locate these two and

I decided to send the first team to arrive to join up with them and get them back to the youth hostel. The second incident was somewhere on the railway line near the top of The Zigzags, where a young soldier from the Royal Army Medical Corps (RAMC) was reported to have gone into a hypothermic coma at 3.00 p.m. It was now 7.00 p.m. and this rescue was going to be a long drawn-out effort. Our information was that there were three other soldiers, including a doctor, with the casualty, and it was thought that they had managed to pitch a tent in a cutting and that the whole party was inside. However, the informant said that one tent had been lost in the gale before they were able to anchor it.

As expected, the RAF Valley team was first to arrive and, after briefing the leader, I left him to run his own show. He set up a base radio in the carpark and, so that we could have uninterrupted communications with the Llanberis team high up on the railway line, the RAF used their own service frequency. I was kept informed about their progress which, because of the conditions, was very slow indeed.

It seemed unbelievable that a forty-six-year-old man would take his two fourteen-year-old sons on to Crib Goch in such severe arctic weather. The steep east ridge of Crib Goch was fully exposed to the gale and they were not properly clothed or equipped to undertake such an expedition. It was not surprising then that the father slipped and fell about 10 metres, or that one of his sons promptly followed him, more or less 'in sympathy'. The information given to us by the son who had not fallen was very worrying, as a man suffering from chest injuries and with breathing difficulties would not stand much chance of surviving for long in a wind-chill of −30°C. We appreciated that his injuries might well prove fatal if he was not rescued quickly, and he certainly would not last the night in that intense cold. The RAF team, aware of this, made every effort to get to the man and his son as quickly as they could. Harvey and Phil had located the casualties and made them as comfortable and warm as possible. I had told them that the RAF boys were on their way to join them, and suggested that as soon as they had taken over the rescue operation, Harvey and Phil should drop down to the Pyg Track and carry on to Bwlch Glas to start searching for the Army group on the railway line.

The rescue of father and son was quite routine and there were no great problems in getting the man securely 'stretchered'. The boy was able to walk down, assisted by a team member. The Pyg Track was very icy and the route from the rock band to Bwlch Moch required a back rope; from the Bwlch to Pen-y-Pass, great care was needed. In normal conditions it would take no more than forty-five minutes – encumbered with a loaded stretcher and with so much ice on the path, it took them nearly four hours to reach the waiting ambulance. The only mention this marathon effort was deemed to merit in the media was ' . . . was brought down by an RAF mountain rescue team'.

Meanwhile I had called out every available member of the Llanberis team and, including the sixteen RAF men, there were forty-eight people actually involved in the two rescues. As soon as the first fifteen Llanberis members arrived, they went off up the Pyg Track to try to make contact with Harvey and Phil who had gone on up to Bwlch Glas. The second group went up the Miners Track in case the Pyg Track proved to be impassable higher up. In fact both routes were passable but not without penalty, for there were deep and soft snowdrifts in many places and it was an exhausting business trying to make headway.

Some members of the Llanberis MRT. Back row (l to r): Aled Taylor, Cledwyn Jones, Nick Walton. Centre row: Sam Roberts, Meirion Thomas, Harvey Lloyd, Hugh Davies, Brede Arkless, Terry Clare, John Grisdale, John Ellis Roberts, Cyril Jones. Front row: Neil Rawlinson & Wilfie, Elwyn Davies, Hugh Walton, Selwyn Davies, Peter Sellers. Aled Taylor, John Ellis Roberts and Hugh Walton have all, in turn, been Chairman of the team. John Grisdale has been secretary for many years.

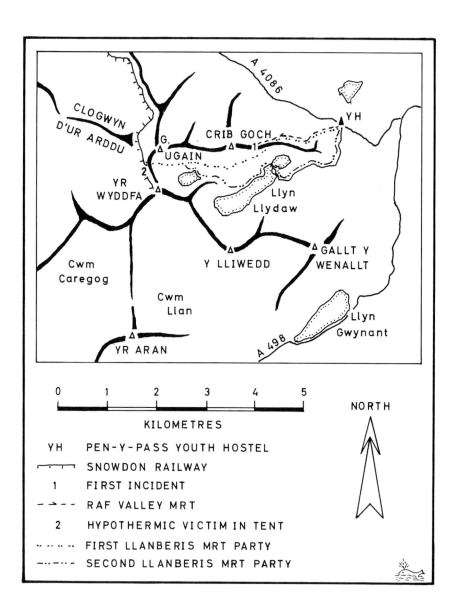

CLOGWYN
D'UR ARDDU

A 4086

YH

G.
UGAIN   CRIB GOCH
1

YR
WYDDFA   2

Llyn
Llydaw

Cwm
Caregog

Y LLIWEDD   GALLT Y
WENALLT

Cwm
Llan

YR ARAN   A 498

Llyn
Gwynant

| 0 | 1 | 2 | 3 | 4 | 5 |

KILOMETRES

NORTH

YH   PEN-Y-PASS YOUTH HOSTEL

⌐—⌐   SNOWDON RAILWAY

1   FIRST INCIDENT

– ➤ – ⋅⋅   RAF VALLEY MRT

2   HYPOTHERMIC VICTIM IN TENT

⋅⋅⋅⋅⋅   FIRST LLANBERIS MRT PARTY

—⋅⋅—⋅⋅   SECOND LLANBERIS MRT PARTY

About an hour after the Miners Track group had set out, I received a radio message that two of the party had turned back and were returning to the youth hostel. The first came into the control room looking ghastly. He was cold and exhausted, and promptly collapsed on the floor. He was revived and re-warmed, but kept under observation until he was fit enough to be taken home. The second man was in a similar state but probably not quite as bad as the first and he recovered more quickly.

The rest of the team pressed on up to The Zigzags and Bwlch Glas, and they eventually located the tent with the four soldiers inside, about five hundred metres down the railway line from the top of The Zigzags. By this time conditions up there were truly horrific. The air temperature was −16°C and the wind was so violent that team members were literally blown off their feet and hurled to the ground. One suffered a fractured humerus just below the shoulder, and another a wrist injury. Two were treated later for minor frostbite to the exposed parts of their faces, and Phil Benbow nearly lost his right big toe due to severe frostbite. Of the rest, one tore ligaments in his knee and another twisted his pelvis when he stepped down into a large drift of powder snow. Altogether nine team members were classified as casualties in the most atrocious weather any of them had ever experienced. With the gale force winds tearing through the air and a temperature of −16°C, the wind-chill effect was reckoned to be approaching −60°C.

As the team turned northwards down the railway line at Bwlch Glas, we lost direct radio communications with them. I had foreseen that this would happen, and had set up a link in Llanberis so that as soon as they went over the ridge on to the railway, we could maintain communications through the link, and never be out of touch. In addition my wife, Anne, at home on the hillside above Waunfawr, was monitoring the rescue on my base set in the sitting room and, on at least two occasions, picked up messages from the team – which for some reason had not been heard, either by link or by myself – and she phoned the information through to me.

It was 11.30 p.m. when the team found the Army tent. The casualty had just regained consciousness after being in a coma for over eight hours. It turned out that the RAMC doctor had recently done a survival course in Norway where he had been taught precisely what to do in this sort of situation, and this undoubtedly saved the young man's life. The condition of the casualty was stabilised and he improved rapidly but, in view of the weather, it was considered best to get him to hospital as speedily as possible. The four km carry-off began soon after midnight and, in the meantime, an ambulance made its way to the end of the metalled mountain road to

Hafodty Newydd. The journey down the mountain was uneventful and, although a helicopter tried to compete with the wind, it was driven backwards and gave up the struggle. At Hafodty Newydd the soldier was transferred into the ambulance and taken to Bangor hospital where he spent a warm and comfortable night – or what remained of it. He was well enough to be discharged back into the Army's care the next day. The two most seriously injured team members who had walked down to the ambulance were taken to hospital with the soldier.

The team had been on the mountain for seven hours, in freezing temperatures, before the last member to come off was checked in at base in Nant Peris. Including those taken to hospital no fewer than nine members reported injuries or exhaustion; in addition, another of the Army group suffered severe frostbite to his fingers.

Meanwhile, the casualty from the Crib Goch incident had been admitted to hospital with suspected broken ribs. The police had contacted his wife at their home and she arrived in Bangor soon after he was admitted. After treatment and a night under observation, he was discharged next morning. Before they left the area, they came round to the rescue team base where I happened to be tidying up and the lady strode in, demanding to know where her husband's rucksack was. She virtually accused someone in the rescue team of stealing the rucksack, which was a disgusting slur on a group of young men who had risked their lives to bring her husband to safety.

The two incidents were given considerable media coverage and the team leaders and National Park wardens were outspoken in their criticism of the irresponsibility and foolhardiness of anyone going out into the mountains in such severe weather. The father in particular was highlighted, as all three of the party were hopelessly ill-prepared for a winter expedition of any sort. It is a sad reflection that the man and his wife would not accept that he had done anything wrong, and a week later a refutation of everything the rescue leaders had said about the ill-conceived expedition appeared in their local paper. Who knows best? Those who spend so much time in the mountains, frequently putting their lives at risk to rescue their fellow human beings, or those who have no worthwhile experience and think it's all too easy? The attitude of the man and his wife was extraordinary, with the accusation that someone in the rescue team had taken the rucksack, and their assertion in the newspaper article that 'we didn't need rescuing, anyway'. One can only hope that when the rucksack was found at the bottom of the slope several weeks later when the snow had melted, they ate humble pie.

First-aid is an Emergency, too

I suppose most people have a pet 'hobby horse' and mine is that one of the most important pieces of equipment in a mountaineer's rucksack is a basic knowledge of practical first-aid. It is a regrettable fact that far too many climbers and walkers venture into remote areas with no knowledge of first-aid whatsoever, thereby putting themselves and their companions at unnecessary risk. It is not simply a matter of knowing what to do to sustain life; it is equally important to know what not to do – as in hypothermia for example. In my view the ordinary first-aid certificate covers the basic principles but does not deal adequately with how to apply them in different environments. It is geared to accidents in the home, on the roads and railways, or on the sports field, but not to the great outdoors. An accident which happens within the environs of a town or village can be speedily dealt with. Local residents will rally round with blankets and mugs of sweet tea, the ambulance will be called and the casualty taken to hospital within a few minutes. Not so in remote hill areas where the all-important factor is time.

If an accident happens, say, two hours' run/walk from the nearest road or telephone, it is likely to be around five hours before a rescue team, which has to be called out and assembled with the necessary equipment, can reach the location of the casualty, and at least another two hours before the stretcher party can rendezvous with the ambulance waiting on the road. In some of our hill or moor-land areas, locally-based Royal Navy or Royal Air Force rescue helicopters can be asked to help, either by dealing directly with the incident themselves or by airlifting rescue teams as near to the casualty as possible. In whichever case, a great amount of vital time will be saved so long as visibility is good enough and a helicopter available. But too much reliance must not be placed on them since, willing as the crews are to help, they may already be committed elsewhere.

The time-lag between an accident happening and the casualty reaching hospital is therefore critical. It is the crux of the whole problem, and it follows that prompt and correct action taken by those on the spot can make all the difference between saving a life and standing by helplessly, watching it ebb away. When confronted with an incident, your adrenalin will start racing round your body, but it is important that you keep calm and, whatever you feel inside, show the casualty and bystanders that you know what you are doing. You should approach the casualty carefully and secure both his and your own position to prevent any further fall. Assess the situation and ascertain whether he is conscious. Since the brain can survive for only about three minutes without oxygen, when a casualty has stopped breathing **every second counts** and the basic ABC routine, which is the same in the mountains as anywhere else, must be carried out immediately.

A is for Airway. Clearing an obstruction of the airway, which may be due to blood, vomit or a swallowed tongue, is the most critical factor in first-aid, especially in head injuries.

B is for Breathing. If breathing has stopped, try to restart it by giving mouth-to-mouth resuscitation. This gets air into the lungs and your exhaled breath has enough oxygen in it to keep a casualty alive.

C is for Circulation. Feel for a pulse. The easiest point is on either side of the throat. If the heart has stopped beating there will be no pulse, and you should try to restart circulation by rhythmically pressing on the casualty's chest (external cardiac massage). This should get blood, carrying oxygen, to the brain without which there will be permanent brain damage within a few minutes. One word of warning – when feeling for a pulse, be very careful before you decide there is not one; there may be an almost imperceptible beat, in which case you must never attempt cardiac massage.

If there is bleeding you must control it as soon as possible by applying pressure over the site. Heavy loss of blood leads to shock which can be a most serious condition. Never give a casualty in shock anything to drink; it may cause vomiting.

Having cleared the airway, all unconscious casualties, except in the case of a suspected broken neck, should be turned into the three-quarters prone position with the mouth lower than the pharynx (the upper part of the gullet or throat). This is called the recovery position and ensures that the tongue will fall forwards, liquid matter will drain away freely, and that the airway will remain open. The recovery position is normally demonstrated on flat ground, but on steep, rocky hillsides this will not be possible. The casualty will have to be positioned on the slope in a slightly head-down posture, and secured by rocks, rucksacks or a rope. A sad example of the reverse of this proper treatment occurs in chapter 13, where those with no knowledge of first-aid had the well-meaning and instinctive reaction to do quite the wrong thing – place the casualty in an upright, sitting position. This story brings out four points. Firstly, that scalp wounds bleed freely, are alarming and look far more serious than they usually are; secondly, that unconscious people should always be put into the recovery position unless a broken neck is suspected; thirdly, that where sufficient people are available, an unconscious person should never be left alone in case he regains consciousness; and fourthly, that only a doctor can certify that a casualty is actually dead, and until that has been done you must carry on as though life can still be saved. In this incident the two men were totally unaware of these points and they were both suffering from shock. They were in no way prepared for what they saw, nor for taking the correct action to try to sustain the girl's life.

ADAPTED RECOVERY POSITION – for any rough or uneven ground such as the rocky slope shown. Manoeuvre the casualty gently into the most comfortable position. Note the use of padding, especially over rocky protrusions. If necessary use rocks or rucksacks to secure the casualty and prevent slipping or rolling down the slope. Author

Heart attacks on the mountain are relatively common and because of the time factor they usually prove fatal. Probably the most susceptible age group is that of thirty-five to fifty years – the family man whose children have reached the age at which he enjoyed his hill-walking. But the fact that it is many years since he was mountain-fit is overlooked by Dad and he sets out for a daylong walk to show his kids what he is made of. Very often Mum does not help either, by providing them with far too much lunch which, after a few hours of climbing upwards, they all tuck into with gusto. It is after the break that trouble begins. Rather than spend extra time for the meal to be digested, they are on their feet too soon and the extra work Dad's heart has to do proves too much and he collapses with a heart attack. Of course not all such attacks are caused in this way, and sometimes they occur to walkers in their eighties. One such incident happened on Snowdon to an eighty-six-year-old lady in late July 1990 when she collapsed in extremely hot weather. Her demise was immediate and I feel sure that is the way she would have chosen to go. However, someone still had the unpleasant job of bringing her body down to the valley.

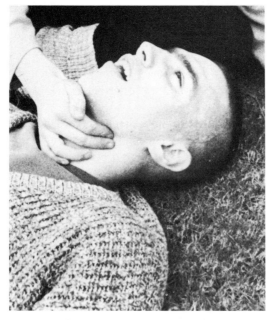

CHECKING THE PULSE IN THE CASUALTY'S NECK – Slide two fingers between the Adam's apple and the thick, firm muscle running up the side of the neck.   *Author*

In the case of a heart attack, if the heart has stopped beating, carry out cardiac massage and artificial respiration (which you must learn on a first-aid course). This must be done within ten minutes of the heart stopping – but the sooner the better – and continued until the patient recovers or is declared dead. If the victim survives the attack, reassure him and make him relax and do absolutely nothing. Put him in the most comfortable position, which is likely to be half-sitting/half-lying, with the shoulders supported and knees bent. The casualty will tell you. Then sit tight until skilled help arrives.

Quite frequently adult teachers or club leaders take groups of young people on mountain expeditions, despite having inadequate or no basic first-aid training. Once learnt, the skills need constant practice and it is important for all those who enjoy going into lonely places to apply the basic principles to that sort of environment. This includes practice in improvising splints, constructing make-shift stretchers from whatever material may come to hand such as gates and old bedsteads, making windproof shelters and so on. Adapting skills to different situations needs initiative and common sense, but not all skills lend themselves to easy adaptation as the following story illustrates.

It is about a teacher who was accompanying a group of young children I was leading down the Miners Track on Snowdon. Between Glaslyn and Llydaw a boy dropped a large piece of quartz on to a girl's foot. She was in a lot of pain, and could not put any weight on the damaged foot: I was fairly sure that one of the tarsal bones had been broken. It was clear that she was not going to be able to walk the three km down to the carpark at Pen-y-Pass, and I was writing out a message to send down to the wardens' centre for assistance, when the teacher, who was bringing up the back-markers of the group, caught up and asked what was happening. I explained the situation to which she replied "Oh, we don't need help, Mr Jones. I've done a first-aid course and we'll carry her off". Bully for you, I thought to myself! "All right then, and how are you going to do that?" I queried. "We'll use the four-handed seat" came the over-confident reply. So I let her get on with it. After no more than twenty paces and nearly dropping the unhappy girl twice, they gave up, and I sent the three most senior boys down with my message. A Land-rover soon appeared and the girl was taken safely and speedily down to wait for an ambulance which arrived within a few minutes. The four-handed seat may be a useful expedient for lifting a casualty off a sports field to the touch-line, but it is out of the question for a long carry down a mountain track.

Learning first-aid in a warm, comfortable environment is very different from applying it 'for real' on a cold windswept hillside amongst all the tension and emotion which a nasty accident evokes. Sometimes even a doctor cannot save a casualty's life, but in many cases the essential knowledge of what to do can be instrumental in keeping the casualty alive until expert medical assistance is available. The important thing is to be able to do **something**; possibly you may chide yourself afterwards for not having done enough, but at least you will have tried.

Hypothermia

It is probably true to say that the majority of mountain incidents are due in some measure to exposure, or to give it a more technical name, hypothermia. It is not my purpose to present a study of this subject, which deals with the ultimate effect of an extreme cold-environment on human beings, in a short book of this sort. For those who wish to delve into the subject, there are whole chapters to be read in various reference books. What I hope to do here is to relate some of my own experiences, and highlight various aspects of hypothermia so that group leaders may be more aware of the insidious nature of the condition and thus take avoiding action, rather than wait until they have a case on their hands with all the trouble and risk it will entail to everyone concerned.

Hypothermia can be immediate, as when a person is immersed suddenly in icy water, in which case it is the acute form; or it can be slow and insidious in its onset, as in the mountains. This is the sub-acute form, and is the subject of this chapter.

The causes of hypothermia come under two headings, environmental and physical. The environmental factors relate principally to dry air temperature and wind speed, which together produce a cooling effect known as WIND-CHILL, an expression being used more frequently nowadays by TV weather-forecasters. In the wind-chill chart opposite, the loss of body heat in a well-clothed person standing still is given for combined air temperature and wind speeds, and a given cooling effect can be read off the chart for different combinations of wind and temperature. In the example given, (the dashed line), the wind-chill effect of an air temperature of 0°C in a 40 km/h wind is −15°C. If the air temperature is −10°C, the same wind-chill effect would be experienced in a windspeed of only 10 km/h. Even a small increase in wind speed, especially up to 25 km/h, produces a marked increase in cooling. Above 25 km/h further increases in wind speed have a relatively lesser effect.

Reference is made to wind-chill in chapter 14, Double Incident, when a full gale combined with a dry air temperature of −16°C produced an estimated wind-chill effect of approaching −60°C.

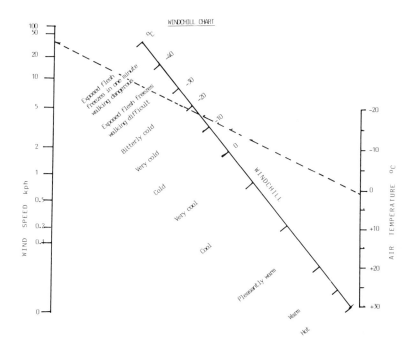

Heat loss is greatly accelerated in wet conditions. Clothing loses a large amount of its insulating properties when it is saturated, particularly if exposed to wind. This is due to evaporation and convection and it is of the greatest importance that hill-walkers and climbers should remain as dry as possible, costly though the most effective waterproof clothing may be. It is money well spent.

The physical factors are really a matter of common sense. Apart from the importance of keeping dry, enough layers of clothing should be worn to keep warm and to afford adequate protection in bad weather. Reserves of energy must be built up before starting out – i.e. eat a good breakfast – and maintained by eating sufficient food during the day, especially if you are walking directly into the teeth of a strong wind, which is extremely exhausting and energy-sapping.

The onset of mountain hypothermia is usually gradual but harmful, the effects compounding themselves as time goes on, and the early signs not easily recognised. Even when there has been no accident, it is a serious danger especially amongst youngsters, the most susceptible age group being the eleven to sixteen bracket. Exposure to bad weather at any time of year, combined with exhaustion, low air temperatures and saturated clothing will cause excessive loss of body heat resulting in a progressive drop in body temperature which, unless correct action is taken, will quickly lead to coma and death. One of the earliest symptoms of hypothermia is a sensation of cold and discomfort felt by the potential victim followed by a dulling of his ability to think clearly. If he fails to react by putting on extra clothing and eating chocolate, for example, it will soon be too late for him to help himself and hypothermia will take over.

It is seldom easy for the group leader or other members of the party to diagnose the condition in its early stages. It calls for much experience and judgement, and a calm, cool approach. Too often assistance is called for, either from a rescue team or a helicopter, when the victim has become exhausted and feels unwell. In many of these cases, a rest out of the wind and a Mars bar or similar, works wonders and enables the walker to make his own way safely off the mountain. It might be said that it is better to over-react rather than leave it too late, but the point is that with experience the leader should be able to differentiate between the person who is just fed up and sees an easy way out, and the genuine case of incipient hypothermia. Over-reaction usually occurs due to lack of experience and leads to a feeling of near-panic, and I would strongly urge all leaders of walking groups, however small, to study and learn well the symptoms of hypothermia, especially in the early stages. These are:–

1. Movements become inefficient, scuffling or dragging of feet, stumbling and slowing of pace;
2. Complaining of coldness, tiredness, shivering and general discomfort including leg cramps;
3. General disinterest in what is going on, i.e. physical and mental lethargy, slowness to understand and answer even simple questions , forgets gloves, compass and increasingly fails to react to commands.

These symptoms are, of course, progressive and with practice a leader will be able to diagnose the onset of hypothermia at earlier and earlier stages of development. One of the later symptoms is seen when cooled blood is circulated to the brain, and the victim displays uncharacteristic behaviour such as physical resistance to help, violent language and violent outbursts of energy, followed by loss of faculties like slurring of speech, vision problems and feeling hot with shedding of clothing, when in fact the core temperature is reaching a dangerously low level.

The first story is about a chance meeting with a group of youngsters in trouble on the summit of Carnedd Ugain. I was doing my weekly walk from Pen-y-Pass to Snowdon summit along the Pyg Track. There was a good deal of snow cover and the weather to start with was fine, clear and very cold. More snow was forecast within a few hours, but I thought I could complete my route before conditions deteriorated. This was not to be, however, and the front came in much more quickly than had been anticipated. By the time I reached the top of The Zigzags the wind had strengthened and it was snowing hard. Visibility was only a few metres.

I decided to make for the summit building and check for any one who might be in difficulty. There were a few people about, but no problems, so I returned to the top of The Zigzags and thence on to Carnedd Ugain. The conditions were even worse by now and I wondered why I was bothering to stay on the high ground rather than look after myself and get back home to a hot bath and tea. It was as well that I was on this particular peak, for I heard voices ahead of me and soon found a party of six youths who were completely lost. I got them together and was about to walk them down to Bwlch Glas when I noticed one of them behaving very strangely. He was wearing a duvet which was unzipped and wide open, and he had no hat or gloves. When I suggested that he should do up his duvet he replied aggressively that he was "too bloody hot". I asked his companions how long he had had his coat open and whether they had noticed anything odd about his behaviour. They thought he had been 'not quite himself' for about half an hour, but he had only just started complaining that he felt too hot. It all added up to advancing hypothermia and I got the whole party into whatever shelter the Pinnacles could offer and commenced re-warming the young man as best we could. We sat it out for an hour or so until the storm eased off a bit, by which time I was satisfied that he was fit enough to walk down to Pen-y-Pass. As usual I had a supply of Mars bars and other chocolate with me, and was able to maintain his energy levels with the occasional nibble all the way down. As it turned out, this incident ended happily but had the youth not been found early enough, or if I had not recognised the symptoms of hypothermia and been able to feed him some energy-giving food, this would certainly have developed into an urgent touch-and-go rescue operation.

The next story goes back in time to November 1978. It was a bitterly cold day and I was acting as a warden up the Pyg Track when a couple of walkers coming down from the summit stopped to report that a woman, whom they thought was American, was walking up ahead wearing open, beach-type sandals. There was some snow on the ground and there was a strong, icy wind from the north-west. The informants were concerned as the woman appeared to be distressed and they thought it likely that she would be in serious trouble. I hastened up the Pyg Track and at the crag where the Pyg and Miners tracks intersect above Glaslyn, I asked several people walking down from the summit if they had seen the woman in sandals. Nobody had, and I assumed that her companions must have taken her down to Glaslyn before I reached the intersection. I continued on my way towards Bwlch Glas, and asked others if they had seen her, but again without result. Several of those I asked, however, told me that a young man was heading for the summit, clad in breeches and shirt, with his socks rolled down, sleeves rolled up and his shirt unbuttoned. Everyone else on the mountain was properly dressed against the biting wind and many expressed irritation at this 'show-off' trying to exhibit a macho image and prove his toughness.

At the top of The Zigzags I met one of the full-time wardens – Aled Taylor – and told him what I had heard. He had just come over Crib-y-Ddysgl and had not seen the man. As he intended to go down the Pyg Track, I said I would go up to the summit and see if the man was still around. There were very few people about when I reached the café building and I thought it was just another wild-goose chase. But I decided to look around, and there he was, out of the wind and being tended by some members of an English mountain rescue team who were there for a change of scenery. The man was already in a polythene bag, with a member of the visiting team in with him.

Aled Taylor.   *John B. Jackson colln.*

The purpose of this is for the warmth of the fit man's body to re-warm the hypothermia victim. I was told that the casualty had collapsed and that they had diagnosed hypothermia and taken the appropriate action.

I introduced myself and asked if they needed any help. I tried unsuccessfully to contact Aled by radio, and then advised them to keep the casualty where he was while I ran down to Pen-y-Pass for help. Their original plan had been to try to walk him down to their base at Rhyd-Ddu, which would take at least an hour and a half, walking straight into the biting wind, as soon as he was fit enough. I urged them not to risk it as I would have help on the way within a couple of hours. In any case as the casualty was bad enough to be in a polythene bag, it was most unlikely that he would recover sufficiently to walk down. The leader of the party assured me that they would stay with the casualty until help arrived, and I 'took off' for Pen-y-Pass.

At about 3.30 p.m., I reported the incident to Aled who was still in the wardens' centre, and the police were informed. A helicopter from 22 Squadron was scrambled, and Aled and I went down to the MRT base at Nant Peris to await its arrival. Two team members were air-lifted and the helicopter made a very thorough search of the summit area and the paths leading down, especially the one to Rhyd-Ddu, but there was no sign of anyone. I was furious. Not only was it extremely risky to move a hypothermia victim within such a short time of his collapse and subsequent re-warming, but to do so after giving me his explicit assurance that he would not move until help arrived was quite deplorable. In the event the helicopter made a useless journey at considerable cost and several people wasted a great deal of time.

I was, of course, closely questioned by the police and I was able to tell them the address given by the rescue team who were looking after the casualty. Two police officers drove round to see if they could find them, and although the casualty was nothing whatever to do with the English party, the police found him in bed in their centre, once again being looked after by his hosts. Apparently he had collapsed, just as I feared he might, on the way down to Rhyd-Ddu, and they had just got him off the hill as the helicopter arrived over the summit. My report of the incident on the summit was thus confirmed and I felt that my credibility had been restored. If there was one lesson to be learned as far as I was concerned, it was that if a request for help is made by people you do not know, it should be made in writing and signed.

Two other points are, firstly, that if I or any other warden had seen the walker dressed as he was, we would have advised him very firmly to cover the exposed parts of his body and, secondly, that once a person has reached the stage of hypothermia where re-warming in a polythene bag has become necessary, he should not be moved until he has fully recovered. Even if he should appear to recover he should always be treated as a stretcher-case and evacuated accordingly. In this case the casualty himself, and the party assisting him, were lucky to get away with it. It was a close-run thing.

A story which highlights the lack of knowledge about the nature and cause of cold-exhaustion and hypothermia relates to a cold, wet day in July 1979. The cloud base was about 850m and I had decided to do a quick two-to-three hour walk from Pen-y-Pass to the 'intersection', going up the Pyg Track, and returning along the Miners Track.

As I came down the scree towards Glaslyn, I met a large party of young schoolchildren varying in age from about ten to sixteen. There were twenty of them, with three leaders in their early twenties. As I approached, I noticed that some of the children looked pale and cold and were sitting around hunched-up and shivering, waiting for their leaders to decide what to do next. They asked me what the weather was like further up the mountain, and would it be alright to take their party up to the summit. I pointed out that the children were already cold and obviously not very happy – which seemed to have escaped their notice – and that they should turn back now and get the group off the hill as quickly as they could. Conditions were colder and wetter higher up and there was no possible reason for pressing on and probably putting all their young charges off hill-walking for life, apart from the obvious danger of some of them becoming hypothermic.

Surprisingly all three leaders accepted my advice without question, and immediately turned the party towards Pen-y-Pass. I felt that they all knew that they should turn back, but none of them wanted to appear timid by being the first to suggest it. What I did not know at this point was that the three were not the real leaders of the group, and that they had been left in charge by two senior lady teachers who had already started back with a sixteen-year-old boy who had seemed to be unwell. Before I left them, the three deputies asked me to keep a look out for the boy and his escorts, who had gone down the Miners Track.

Just past the crushing mill on Llyn Llydaw, I spotted a lone walker ahead of me. He was walking very slowly and seemed to be dragging his feet, so I lengthened my stride to catch up with him. As I drew level, a sideways glance showed me a pale, almost grey complexion and a complete lack of expression on his face. I asked if he was all right, and a slurred answer indicated that he was cold, tired and fed up. Was he alone, I asked and a floppy hand pointed out two female walkers who had come into view about two hundred metres in front of us. "They are my teachers," the boy said.

Even to someone with only a little knowledge of hypothermia, it must have been obvious that the boy was on the verge of becoming a victim, and at this stage his cold exhaustion was already producing symptoms which should have sounded the alarm bells. His speech, pallor and lack of interest in what was happening around him, together with the shuffling of his feet were all signs of the onset of hypothermia. I gave him a Mars bar to eat, and told him to sit down and rest for a few minutes while I went ahead to speak to his teachers. Chocolate bars like Mars are often very effective at this stage, but it is vital that they are eaten before the potential victim has lost interest in his own condition, and also the will to do anything about it anyway. I drew level with the two women who were deep in conversation, oblivious of everything around them. I bade them 'Good morning' and asked if they were anything to do with the young lad behind them. They looked back and then chorused "Oh him – yes, he's all right – just a bit tired." I was speechless for a moment then, regaining my composure, I suggested politely that he was not all right and that he was near to collapse with hypothermia. There was a gale of laughter from both teachers followed by "Hypothermia? You can't get hypothermia in July!" It really was almost unbelievable, and having corrected their misapprehension as politely as I could, I went back to fetch the boy, and told the two teachers to walk him down to Pen-y-Pass, get him inside the café and give him a hot drink.

About an hour later I saw the boy sitting hunched-up on the ground outside the café and I asked him if he had been inside and had something hot to drink. I think I knew the answer before he gave it to me. His teachers had told him to wait there for the rest of the group to come off the hill, and as far as he knew, they themselves had gone inside. I was rightly incensed, and took him inside to give him the drink he needed. We sat down at a table next to where the two women were once again discussing something quite unrelated to what they were presumably being paid to do. Clearly they still firmly believed that 'you can't get hypothermia in July,' and no one was going to persuade them otherwise.

Navigation is Fun

Navigation is fun, but nevertheless it is a serious business and is no laughing matter when things begin to go wrong. It is a sobering thought that many mountain incidents are due to errors in navigation somewhere along the line. The advice to 'always take your map and compass with you' is fine as far as it goes. It presumes that you know how to use them properly – and that does not just mean knowing how to walk on a given bearing: it means being able to work out a day's route, estimating distance and time for each section so that you arrive at your destination well before dark – and much more besides. The ability to prepare a route-card should ensure that you will never make the common mistake of being over-ambitious and possibly becoming benighted. It will also remind you to plan escape routes so that if necessary you can abort your planned walk and follow a safe route to lower ground.

A few years ago we were called out to look for an elderly couple who had not returned to the hostel for supper. They had left no indication of where they had intended to walk, and the only clue was that another guest at the hostel thought he had seen them near the summit of Snowdon at lunch-time, but he could not be sure. It was mid-August, the time was 8.00 p.m. and there was still an hour or so of daylight left. The search dogs were asked to cover the main paths to the summit and it was almost dark when my navigator and I found the two old people walking towards Snowdon up the Miners Track above Llyn Llydaw. They were quite disorientated and thought they were heading for Nant Gwynant. "Haven't you got a map?" I asked. "Yes, but the maps of this area don't show the footpaths," the old man replied as he pulled a tattered old road map from his pocket! It was an extreme example of a hill-walker taking 'his map with him' without the slightest idea how to use it.

Even experienced walkers can be guilty of complacency and, because they are on familiar ground, leave the map in a pocket and rely on their 'sense of direction'. If that means that you have a built-in radar which automatically points you in the right direction, there is no such thing in my book, as I learned the hard way many years ago in an incident on Snowdon. It nearly resulted in a disastrous accident involving a party of six youths led by me.

One keynote to safe route-finding is to work out distances and bearings before setting out. It is much easier and will be done more accurately in the comparative warmth of a tent or hut than on a freezing, gale-swept hillside. Sometimes, however, you may have to do the map work in unpleasant conditions and if this happens take care to be as accurate as you can, for any errors you make may well result in serious difficulties.

Not long ago I was walking down to Llanberis from Snowdon summit when I chanced upon a party of walkers midway between the top of Parsley Fern Gully, SH 610553 and the ruined stables at SH 608558. There was deep, fresh snow on the ground, and hill fog limited visibility to only a few metres. The group was heading down towards and across the Llanberis path which was, of course, under several inches of snow. Their trilby hats, overcoats and umbrellas marked them as a city party, and there was no hesitation in stopping them to ensure that they knew what they were doing: I could see that their direction of travel was straight towards the iced-up cutting at Clogwyn Goch. I asked the leader where they were heading for, and when he replied "Clogwyn station" I knew I was right to offer help. "I'm sorry," I said, "but you're way off course. Can we just check your bearings?"

He produced his map case, a smooth, slippery plastic one which he held in one hand and placed his compass on it. Trying to keep the map flat, he measured the grid bearing from where he thought he was, but his true position was almost two hundred metres to the south. He then put that bearing on the compass, forgot to add the six degrees west magnetic variation, and that was the direction in which he was leading the group. The extra six degrees would have taken him well to the right of Clogwyn Goch, though not far enough to avoid the steep side of the railway-cutting back-wall. Apart from that common mistake regarding magnetic variation, his method of taking the grid bearing was slipshod and inaccurate. The compass slipped on his map case, and I persuaded him to place the map on the ground or on a rock, and to use both hands to keep the compass steady. We went through the procedure again and came up with a magnetic bearing seventeen degrees west of the one he had been following, and this took them safely to Clogwyn station.

Just to have your map and compass with you is not sufficient, you must learn how to use them correctly, and the more you practise the more proficient you will become. Always double-check that you have remembered to add or subtract the Magnetic Variation and finally, when you have done all this and are confident that you have worked out the bearings and distances correctly, trust your compass. Then navigation really will be fun, and there is

A well-equipped group of boys enjoying a navigation exercise on Foel Grach.   *Author*

nothing which will give you more satisfaction than arriving at the right place at the right time at the end of a day-long expedition.

British Ordnance Survey maps provide almost all the information needed to plan a route, except for one vital thing, which was brought home to me on the Cairngorms in the mid-sixties. I had planned a route from Achlean (sheet 36 1:50,000, NN852976), following the path to NN893968, then across country to The Angels Peak (NN955976), Cairn Toul (NN962972), pt 1213 (NN963962) and returning via the bend in the track at NN911957. The estimated distance was 25km, with 1350 metres of ascent for which, using a revised Naismith's formula[1], I allowed 7 and 3 hours respectively, a total of 10 hours.

It was a hot, sunny day and we started walking at 7.00 a.m. with our expected return at 5.00 p.m. However, once we had left the path and headed towards the ridge overlooking Loch Einich, we were on very broken, boggy ground with constant climbing in and out of deep peat-hags for some 3½ km. This ground not only slowed our rate very considerably but also exhausted us so much that we could not maintain our 4 km/h once we were

---

[1] 4 km/h for horizontal distance and one hour for every 450 metres of ascent. Over the years I have found this formula to be more relevant to occasional and unfit walkers.

clear of the hags. Although we headed further south than we had intended, towards Tom Dubh (NN921953) and Pt. 876m on our way back – thus avoiding the boggy area – by the time we reached the track, we were so tired that it was a case of dragging one foot after the other. From there, it was nearly all downhill and we made it safely back, but it had taken us 3½ hours longer than we had planned, we were late for supper and there was concern for our safety.

With experience you will learn that high plateaux giving rise to streams and lochans, e.g. Llyniau in Wales, are almost certain to be areas of peat-hags and very difficult going. But maps cannot indicate such conditions, and my advice to anyone planning a high-level cross-country route is to ask someone with local knowledge.

When it comes to teaching youngsters how to navigate, the aim should be to do some pre-planned routes as early as possible in their training to prove that map and compass really can be relied on to get them safely to their destination.

False Alarms

People who love the mountains have always seemed to me to be a breed in which, very often, the finest traits of the human character are revealed, yet it is surprising that people who one day will devote time and effort to assist a fellow mountaineer in difficulty, perhaps at considerable risk to themselves, will next day do something which puts their colleagues to needless inconvenience and exposure to harm. My time in MR has been punctuated with examples of incidents of this sort, a short selection of which are included in this chapter.

The first such false alarm happened on Friday April 18th 1982 when a twenty-five-year-old school teacher from London set out from the Snowdon Ranger Youth Hostel to walk to the summit of Snowdon and then make his way down to the Llanberis Youth Hostel where he had pre-booked a bed and an evening meal. When he failed to arrive, the warden informed the police, and the Llanberis MRT was asked to assist. At about 10.00 p.m. the three local SARDA dog handlers were briefed and deployed to search the most likely areas. These included all the possible routes from the youth hostel to Snowdon summit along the Ranger Path, over the Moel Eilio ridge to Llanberis, via Bwlch Maescwm to Llanberis, and up the railway line and Llanberis path (two routes) from Llanberis to the summit. The search lasted all night and by morning there was hardly a square metre of this extensive area which had not been covered. But there was no sign of the missing teacher and at first light on the Saturday morning the Llanberis MRT, supported by a RAF helicopter, joined the search as the SARDA teams were being withdrawn for food and rest.

As always on these occasions, the police had informed their counterparts in the missing man's home town – London – but although they visited his house periodically during the night, they got no reply and reported that he was not there. Whilst over 40 searchers were still out looking for him, the man was apprehended by the police at about 9.00 a.m. on Saturday morning as he walked out of his front door, closely followed by his girl friend. No wonder the police had not been able to get a reply! As soon as the information came through to Llanberis, the search was called off.

It transpired that the teacher had made good progress on his walk to the summit and had arrived at the Youth Hostel in Llanberis at around 3.00 p.m., two hours before the hostel opened at 5.00 p.m. He decided on the spur of the moment to pack up and go back to London. He made his way to Bangor and caught a train for London, arriving there sometime late in the evening, but by this time the search for him was already in progress. As John Grisdale, secretary of the Llanberis MRT, told the Press, "The man we were searching for should have telephoned a youth hostel or the police before leaving the area. He broke one of the golden rules of mountaineering by going off without telling anyone." He could also have left a written message at the Llanberis YH, but he did neither. The irritation felt by team members was compounded by the man's lack of contrition.

Almost seven years later a copy-book incident occurred, again involving the Llanberis team. It was the morning of Friday April 14th 1989, when a 17-year-old youth, whom we'll call Joe, was found asleep in his garden shed in Coventry whilst a massive search for him was taking place in Snowdonia.

Joe had spent the Wednesday night in a Llanberis hotel where he had booked in for four nights, and on Thursday morning he told the hotelier he was going to walk to the summit of Snowdon. The hotelier rightly advised him not to go as he was not equipped or adequately clothed for the wintry conditions high up, but Joe left the hotel about mid-morning and was seen heading towards the mountains. I was leading a party of YTS trainees on Snowdon that day with my colleagues Roland Layland and Neil Rawlinson, and none of us made it to the summit as we were floundering in deep snow which in places was waist deep. We gave it best and turned for home at about 1.00 p.m. Meantime Joe had not gone on to the mountain at all, but made his way back to Coventry, leaving some of his belongings in his hotel room, and his bill unpaid. He spent the evening drinking with friends, and when he locked himself in the garden shed for the night, the search for him was being set in motion in Snowdonia. All the indications were that he had in fact gone up the mountain, and in view of the conditions we had experienced up there earlier in the day, there was genuine concern for the young man's safety.

By midnight the Llanberis MRT had become involved, and initially SARDA was asked to provide three dog teams. At 1.30 a.m. they were airlifted to a height of approximately 600 metres by an RAF helicopter from Valley. Above 750 metres progress became very slow due to the depth of snow, but the dog teams, which included Roland and Neil, struggled on, covering all the most likely places where Joe might have fallen, whilst throughout the night avalanches crashed down from the melting cornices.

'Into action': Roland Layland and Toby, followed by Bob Maslen-Jones and Gelert embarking at Pen-y-Pass.   Clive Swombow

For all three handlers it was a frightening experience. At first light both the Llanberis and RAF Valley MRTs were deployed on and around Snowdon, whilst the helicopter, having airlifted the teams as high up the mountain as possible, was methodically over-flying the area. By 9.00 a.m. more than fifty ground searchers, six dog teams and the helicopter were involved in the operation. Many of the civilian team members had taken time off work and would lose a day's pay.

Back in Coventry the police were constantly checking Joe's home. His mother spent a sleepless night worrying about her son, unaware that he was asleep in the garden shed, where she found him at about 10.00 a.m. on Friday morning. When told that a huge search for him was going on, Joe said "I don't know what all the fuss is about. I didn't ask anyone to go searching for me."

Rescue teams throughout Britain will find nothing new in this reaction. It is a sort of self-defence retort, and is very common. Only two or three years before this incident a party of schoolboys from the south-east, under the leadership of their master, left their rucksacks containing all their survival gear in 'Jean's Hut' (now demolished) in Coire an Lochain while they did an ice-climb up to the Cairngorm plateau. Up there it was a white-out and the leader set off on a compass bearing in a totally wrong direction. After a while, in his own words, they were "navigating by the seat of our pants." The group somehow found its way to Loch Avon and managed to follow the shore of the loch, then through a narrow pass into Strath Nethy, eventually reaching Bynack Stable bothy at 3.00 a.m.

By this time all the stops were being pulled out as, in the very raw conditions, there was great concern for the well-being of the boys. Without food and extra clothing they could have been at serious risk, and rescue teams, search dogs and helicopters, plus volunteers were quickly mobilised and deployed on to the plateau as they reported for duty.

The party stayed in the bothy until daylight, then made its way the short distance to Glenmore Lodge where the search was being co-ordinated. When told that already more than fifty people, as well as search dog teams and two helicopters were out looking for them, the leader angrily retorted that he had not asked them to go "chasing round the mountains looking for him", and anyway they had arrived back safely so what was the fuss all about? The search co-ordinator cut him down to size by pointing out that the concern was for six young boys under a leader whose ability was very much in doubt. It was a matter of sheer luck that they had managed to find their way in the dark, with all footpaths obliterated by snow, and he could not claim any credit for his navigation.

Not everyone who is reported missing on the hills adopts the same self-centred attitude. For example, in October 1988, a middle-aged couple walking in the hills and forests of mid-Wales somehow got lost. They had experience of walking in many countries, and they had left word at their hotel of roughly where they intended going, and said that they would definitely be back for dinner. When they failed to return, the local police were informed and by midnight the local MRT and every available search dog had been committed to the search for the missing couple. Meanwhile, with little spare clothing, empty flasks and nothing more than a chocolate bar or two for food, the couple settled down in the depths of the forest to spend a cold and utterly miserable night. By the early hours they were not in good shape and were becoming concerned for their survival. Shortly after 5.00 a.m. John Burson's German Shepherd bitch, Tammy, picked up their scent and as soon as it was light enough, John led them safely down to the nearest road.

This incident ended happily and the couple will forever be thankful that there were volunteers ready to give up a night's sleep and spend the hours of darkness out on the hills when the call came. The outcome could easily have been different, and most certainly would have been if the rescue services had ignored the concern of the hotelier. Such was the couple's gratitude that immediately after leaving the police station they went to the MRT base and made a generous donation to the team's funds; then they did the same for SARDA, and they continue to support the Association today.

The great majority of people who go missing, or are injured or stuck on a rock face, are extremely pleased and relieved to be brought to safety. But now and then the selfish side of human nature asserts itself and after being rescued the 'victims' tell their rescuers "Thanks very much, but we were quite all right really and we didn't ask to be rescued." It may be that there are people yet who think that they might be asked to pay for their rescue as is the case almost everywhere else in the world, but not in Britain.

Mountain Rescue Teams have to answer quite a number of false alarms; some are genuine mistakes and are accepted with good grace, but others, due to irresponsibility, carelessness or sheer thoughtlessness, are inexcusable and cause a great deal of annoyance to the services. Probably one of the most irritating types of false alarm is when someone has left a route-card with a clearly stated return time, and then goes somewhere else without bothering to tell anyone, as the following anecdote illustrates.

At our hotel in Llanberis, in March 1983, two young climbers filled in one of the route-cards I provided, stating that after doing a quick climb on the Gromlech they would leave their car at Pen-y-Pass and walk the 'Horseshoe'. They expected to be back at the hotel by 6.00 p.m. Having started at 9.15 a.m. this gave them 8 hours to complete their planned route. The weather was dry with cloud down to 800 metres, and when the men had not returned by 7.30 p.m., I thought that as they had not previously done the 'Horseshoe', they could well have missed the path coming down from Lliwedd in the fog and have continued straight on to Gall-y-Wenallt and become lost. The staff at the Pen-y-Pass Youth Hostel checked the carpark, but their car was not there so I informed Operations Room at Police HQ that the two men were overdue, and suggested that they should have all the lay-bys and carparks round the Snowdon massif checked by patrol cars. This was promptly carried out, but with negative results.

At 9.00 p.m., while the police patrol cars were doing their check, my daughter Liz was walking through Llanberis and telephoned to say that there were two young men having a meal in the Chinese restaurant and she thought they might be our missing guests. It had begun to look more and more likely that we were going to have to search the whole of the Snowdon

Horse-shoe route, but before we started to call out the MRT and SARDA, I asked the police in Llanberis if they could check whether the two men in the Chinese restaurant were the two we were seeking. They were, and following a reasoned but very firm dressing-down from the police sergeant, they came back to the hotel very contrite and profuse in their apologies. They did not make any excuses and admitted that they had changed their minds after doing the route on the Gromlech and decided to drive to Tremadoc and climb down there. It had never occurred to either of them to let us know as both of them had completely forgotten that they had left a route card.

But for a stroke of luck, and Liz's vigilance, within another half-hour or so a lot of people would have been called out and a major search operation set in motion.

Usually a telephone call is all that is required to let someone know that you are safely off the mountain, albeit in the wrong valley, or that you have changed your plan and have decided to go home instead. Just ten pence could save wasting many thousands of pounds, quite apart from needless risk to rescuers. In this country the police are responsible for the safety of civilians, and whenever they are given information which suggests that someone might be in trouble in some wild, desolate place, they are duty-bound to take suitable action. They will first seek the advice of the local MRT leader and, having decided on a course of action, they will then co-operate with the team in whatever search or rescue operation is carried out. Nobody ever asks to be looked for. It is done as a matter of course and those who bleat so self-righteously that they "don't know what all the fuss is about" would be the first to shout, "Where's the mountain rescue?" if they were lying out there with a broken ankle and nobody bothered. They really cannot have it both ways.

Indifferent Leadership

The headline in the *Daily Mail* on May 4th 1982 was brief and succinct. It read 'Mistakes on the Killer Mountain', and most other national dailies carried the same story at some length. A party of thirty-eight Scouts aged between 13 and 17, which included four girls and seven adult leaders, one of whom had never been on Snowdon before, set out from their home base in the Midlands on Friday April 30th to climb Snowdon over the weekend as part of a Duke of Edinburgh's Award and Queen's Scout Award exercise. The expedition leader had listened to a telephoned weather forecast sometime that evening after which, having moved off into the mountains to camp, there was no means of getting an update on it. Whilst a transistor radio is not a recommended item to be carried on expeditions and as far as I know is not suggested in any mountain walking literature, a small lightweight set, not to blare pop music across the mountains but to keep up to date on changes in weather forecasts, is not a bad idea as was illustrated one Easter weekend early in the 1970s. A group of four boys started their Duke of Edinburgh 50-mile expedition on Good Friday morning from Capel Curig in bright sunshine, and some three hours later they were lost in a complete and sudden white-out with over 15 centimetres of snow on the ground over 900 metres up on the Carneddau. They pitched their tent and waited for conditions to improve, and in the meantime one of the boys switched on his small transistor to help while away the time. As concern for their safety grew the boy's father broadcast messages of encouragement to the lads over the BBC, telling them to stay in their tent, and that a search for them was already in operation. The boys heard the messages, did as they were told, and five days later when the cloud lifted they were found safe and well.

In the 1982 incident no one had a transistor radio with him, and the leader said, "I checked the weather forecast on the telephone on Friday night and it was for wind and showers, becoming brighter on Sunday." That forecast was already eighteen hours old as the telephone forecast tape is prepared at 6.00 a.m. each day from a special Snowdonia National Park forecast issued by Cardiff Weather Centre. But at the time it was the best forecast the leader could get, and he had added that on the basis of that forecast he had assumed that the weather would get better. During Saturday the party carried out various exercises at low level and camped for the night near Llyn Ffynnon-y-Gwas close to the Snowdon Ranger Path, and the weather remained much as forecast until about 9.00 a.m. on Sunday.

I make a point of listening to the weather forecast as often as I can because in the mountains, especially along a seaboard, it changes frequently and rapidly. Forecasts are not always accurate as British mountains are something of a law unto themselves and tend to have their own micro-climates. A blanket forecast therefore cannot hope to be accurate for such areas every time, but with experience you can interpret the general trend of the weather pattern and get a reasonably good idea of what to expect.

The outlook forecast for North Wales on that Saturday morning was for a sudden and dramatic change soon after breakfast on Sunday. Gales gusting to more than 70 mph accompanied by torrential rain, hail, sleet and snow on the highest ground was to be the mixture, and it was a complete U-turn from the forecast the leader had heard on Friday night. During Saturday night the Scouts slept blissfully unaware of what was in store for them next morning. Sunday started much the same as Saturday and after breakfast they struck camp and set off in small groups, each group with an adult leader, up The Zigzag section of the Snowdon Ranger Path heading for the summit of Snowdon. It was then about 10.00 a.m.

At much the same time I told my wife that I was going to take the dogs out for some exercise up the Llanberis path, that I would be out for an hour or so before the expected storm hit us, and that I would be back for lunch. I drove up to the start of the path at Cader Ellyll and saw dark menacing clouds forming and swirling viciously round the summit. The storm was ahead of schedule and was about to break and, as there was no-one about, I changed my plan and went up to Pen-y-Pass instead. In spite of the forecast the carpark was full. In the wardens' information centre Aled Taylor, one of the full-time wardens who had his leg in plaster following an unfortunate fall which resulted in a badly broken ankle, was on duty. I asked him where everyone had gone. "I've warned as many as I could about the weather," he said, "but they've all gone up the Pyg or Miners Tracks, presumably to see what a real storm is like." "OK Aled," I replied, "are there any other wardens up there?" He told me there were not, and I decided to walk up the Miners Track to Glaslyn as I felt sure some of the walkers would be in trouble. "I'll be back about tea-time," I told him and, after telephoning Anne to tell her of my change of plan, I topped up my supply of Mars bars from the café and set off into the rising storm.

It was not long before I met the first of the walkers coming down. The storm had developed with frightening speed and before long the Miners Track looked like the retreat from Moscow, as saturated but cheerful groups, thoroughly enjoying the experience, made their way back to their cars. I struggled on into the gale and it took me almost two hours to reach Glaslyn – twice my usual time. The stream of refugees had dwindled to the odd group by this time, and at the ruined barracks I asked what seemed to be the last group if they had seen anyone behind them. They had not and, as they had been almost to the summit, they were fairly sure they were the last to come down. They went on their way and I decided to eat a Mars bar before turning for home. It was now about 1.30 p.m. and after a short rest in the shelter of the ruins I stood up and got ready to move off. A last glance up the steep boulder-strewn path revealed some shapes just visible through the driven sleet, slowly feeling their way down to the lake.

It was clear that the group, five of them in all, was not in good shape and as the leading member cleared the last of the rock he stumbled and fell ten metres down the scree. "Oh, God," I said to myself, "that's all I need," and picking up my rucksack I ran the fifty metres to where he was lying motionless. His face was ashen and he did not appear to be breathing. I felt his carotid pulse which was strong enough, and as I opened his mouth to make sure his airway was clear he suddenly drew in a deep breath, gurgled loudly, and soon recovered. He had winded himself but otherwise was none the worse for his fall.

The rest of the group of three Scouts and two adult leaders had caught up by now and told me they had walked over from Llanberis *en route* for Pen-y-Pass. They were very cold and wet and I suggested that they should eat something before making their way down. "We didn't bring any food with us," they said, "as we thought we would be able to get something to eat in the café at Pen-y-Pass." I was staggered by this admission, but I was concerned about their condition for they had seemed to be nearly exhausted as they made their way down the boulder path. Luckily I had bought enough Mars bars before I set out, and I gave them one each which I reckoned would be enough to get them to the carpark. They were very grateful and we set off together down the Miners' Track. I learned from one of the leaders that they had in fact heard the weather forecast, but he said "we never thought it would be anything like as bad as this." In spite of the Mountain-walking Leaders Certificate (MLC), it seems that even the most careful organisations sometimes send youngsters into the mountains under the leadership of adults whose enthusiasm exceeds their experience.

Just below Glaslyn we met a party of six boys from a Boys' Club making their way up the mountain. I left the Scout group to carry on down, intending to catch them up when I had spoken to this other group and found out where they were going. The 17-year-old leader said he was in charge of a Duke of Edinburgh Award expedition and they were going to camp near the summit of Snowdon. "Oh no you're not," I said, "I suggest that you either camp down here or go back to your base." "We can't do that," said the leader, "Skip told me that under no circumstances are we to change the plan." Fully aware that I had no authority to order anyone to do anything, I said "Well, I'm ordering you to return to Pen-y-Pass (which was their only possible escape route anyway) and I will tell your Skip why." "Thank you, sir," replied the boy, "this storm is really scary and we're all wet and tired already." I looked at the group, a motley lot, and noticed that the smallest boy was carrying a big frame rucksack which reminded me of a huge spinnaker jib dwarfing the yacht which carried it. I could imagine the lad being blown into space by the gusts on the ridge higher up. I couldn't possibly allow them to continue. As we started down towards Llyn Llydaw, a violent gust hit us from behind and sent the little lad sprawling. He was badly shaken and somewhat demoralised, but unhurt. For the rest of the walk down I held his hand to give him stability and reassurance. On the way down towards Pen-y-Pass, I thought about the two groups I had met and came to the conclusion that in both cases the indifferent leadership of the adult leaders was due to lack of experience, especially about the severity of mountain weather. In the first case, it seemed incredible that adult leaders in charge of someone else's children could listen to such a clear weather warning and then virtually disregard it because they did not think conditions could be so bad. To compound this mistake, the two leaders must have known that their route would take them at least four hours, and to set out, especially having heard the forecast, with no food whatsoever was remarkably irresponsible. When I met them again in the carpark, I told them what I thought of their leadership, and I can only hope that they took it to heart and did not venture out again until they became properly organised. Unfortunately I never met Skip, as I was ready to tell him in uncompromising terms that I thought his instruction to his young leader not to turn back under any circumstances was completely wrong and irresponsible. What, pray, are escape routes for? To appoint a leader and then deny him the option to exercise his initiative and seek safer ground if conditions so dictate, was surely a very serious error of judgement and placed the boy in a very vulnerable position.

In the meantime, how had the Scouts from the Midlands been faring? When I saw the clouds racing in and swirling round the summit at 10.00 a.m., they had just started their main ascent. The wind was blowing from right to left across the general direction in which they were walking, causing no great problems until they had crossed the plateau at the top of the Ranger Path zigzags, when they swung righthanded and found themselves walking directly into the gale. The small groups pressed on towards the summit and assembled there at about 1.00 p.m., and at this time everyone was accounted for.

Exactly what happened then is not clear as there was some contradiction in the statements made later to the police and press reporters by members of the party and group leaders. The expedition leader's explanation was that he had made a wrong assumption, for he believed that the snow would be coming from the north and he therefore led the party down the south ridge into the teeth of the gale. But what snow? He had already said that the only forecast he had heard, on Friday night, spoke of wind and showers, becoming brighter on Sunday. So when did he hear about the snow, and with the gale already blowing from the south, how could the snow be blown in from the opposite direction? One can only assume that the front carrying the snow would move in from the north, but the snow itself would be blown directly into their faces from the south. To make things even worse he pleaded that "we could never have expected such dramatic weather." In mountains there is no limit to the severity of the conditions, and leaders especially should not be taken too much by surprise if unexpectedly they do find themselves beset by 'dramatic' weather. Be that as it may, the die was cast and the party set off down the south ridge in their small groups, but trying to keep together as much as they could. Across Bwlch Main they made painfully slow progress against what were now storm-force winds and blinding snow. They became badly strung out and the last group of six boys lost contact with their adult leader and the rest of the party, split into two smaller groups and quickly lost contact with each other. The whole expedition was now out of control, and so exhausted had the boys become that they jettisoned much of their equipment to lighten their loads and left it lying on the ridge to be blown over the cliffs into Cwm Tregalan. Some of the Scouts managed to make their way down to the road at Rhyd-Ddu, and others went down into Nant Gwynant where they raised the alarm. The National Park wardens responded immediately to the emergency and were soon busy helping to round up the stragglers and get them safely off the hill. It was now about 4.00 p.m.

It was shortly before this that I reached the carpark and was looking forward to a good tea and hot bath before opening the bar in the hotel. As I approached the wardens' centre Sam Roberts came out to meet me. "Thank God you're back, Bob," he said. "I've got reports coming in of large numbers of Scouts scattered all over the other side of the mountain. As far as I can make out there are twenty not accounted for, and those who have got down to the road are in various stages of hypothermia, so God knows what those still out there are like. Gareth is in the Rhyd-Ddu area with John Jackson (a voluntary warden) but we've not got any direct radio communications, so if you can stay and run things from here, I'll go round to Rhyd-Ddu which seems to be where the bulk of the boys are coming down, and Aled can drive down to Pont Bethania and open up a radio link there. We should be able to talk round the mountain like that." "OK, Sam, who has been informed so far?" I asked. "No one yet," he replied. "It has only just started, but it looks very serious and I should put the team on stand-by until we get some definite information about numbers actually missing."

Page 1 of my log starts the tale:

Hugh Walton and Harvey Lloyd to put their teams on stand-by.

Tony Jones, Ogwen Valley MRT, informed of incident and asked to put his team on stand-by and to inform RAF MRT and C Flight 122 Squadron helicopters that they could well be needed as soon as the gales abated.

In fact both the 'Oggie' team and a helicopter were involved in a very hazardous rescue on Tryfan and it was likely to be some time before they would be able to assist. The radio set-up worked well and for the next forty-five minutes messages indicated that the Scouts were finding their way off the hill in twos and threes, but still no firm figure of the number yet adrift could be given. At 5.00 p.m. the number of the original party was given as forty with seven still not accounted for. Forty minutes later the number of missing was reduced to six.

It was at about this time that a woman walker found two of the Scouts from the leaderless rear group in Bwlch-y-Llan. They were in a very bad way, and having done all she reasonably could for them, she raced off to get help, meeting wardens Gareth Davies and John Jackson making their way up the old quarry track from Rhyd-Ddu to Bwlch-y-Llan in a Land-rover. She told them about the two boys, one of whom was in a critical condition and whom she had tried to get into a polythene bag. The other was just about able to walk but was extremely cold and was, she thought, already hypothermic. As Gareth and John searched for the two boys, I received the news over the radio and informed the police of this serious development. Warden Sam Roberts had been alerted and made his way round from Pont Bethania in his Land-rover. He drove up the track towards Bwlch-y-Llan where he joined Gareth and John.

When they were found, the older of the two boys, a seventeen-year-old Venture Scout, was unconscious. He was given mouth-to-mouth resuscitation and carried as carefully and gently as possible to the Land-rover, and then taken down to a waiting ambulance at Rhyd-Ddu. Sadly he was dead on arrival at Bangor hospital, but his companion recovered.

Back in the wardens' centre at Pen-y-Pass, I had been joined by another voluntary warden, Meirion Thomas, who was also a member of the Llanberis MRT. Meantime I was able to monitor what was happening over the mountain fairly accurately and kept Hugh Walton and Harvey Lloyd informed of progress. It was 6.30 p.m. before the two hypothermic boys were in the ambulance and on the way to hospital in Bangor, and as soon as I knew they were mobile, I telephoned the senior casualty officer, Dr Ieuan Jones, who was also the Honorary Medical Officer of the Llanberis MRT, and gave him all the information I could about the incident. Their expected arrival time at the hospital was 7.15 p.m., which gave the casualty department advance warning. Possibly this was instrumental in saving the second boy's life.

My main preoccupation was to get confirmation of the exact number, if any, of the Scouts who were still missing. Every available MRT and all the SARDA teams had been on stand-by for two hours and I wanted to give them all a firm decision to stand-down or turn out before much longer. There was so much confusion that at one stage no one seemed to know how many people had been in the party to start with! However, at 6.07 p.m. I received a message that four boys aged from thirteen to fifteen were definitely not accounted for, and that they were on their own without an adult leader. They were the second part of the rear group of six, one of which had already died from hypothermia, and this caused us all very serious concern. Meirion and I then called out all those on stand-by to report to Pen-y-Pass urgently.

At about 6.45 p.m. I put Hugh Walton and Harvey Lloyd fully in the picture and, as all the action was taking place around Rhyd-Ddu, Hugh decided that the search base should be moved there. By the time he arrived in the village, the police had arranged for the old school house to be used as base, and in the meantime Meirion and I, at Pen-y-Pass, redirected everyone to Rhyd-Ddu. Satisfied that all those who had been on stand-by had reported, I closed down at the wardens' centre at 7.15 p.m. and went back to the hotel to feed the dogs. I got myself some sandwiches and refilled my flask for by now I had been called out as a dog handler! My two-hour walk – 'back for lunch' – had already lasted nine hours and looked like going on throughout the night.

I reported to Phil Williams-Jones, our Chairman, who was co-ordinating the SARDA operation from Rhyd-Ddu, at 8.30 p.m. and he asked me to drive round to Pont Bethania and search up the Watkin Path into Cwm-y-Llan to meet up with dog teams which would be converging at the bwlch where the two Scouts had been found earlier. These teams would have covered the ground to the west of South Ridge up on to the ridge itself. Because of my involvement at Pen-y-Pass I was the last of the dog handlers to arrive, and Phil followed me round to the start of the Watkin. He then set up a radio link on the rising ground about 1 km south of the main road, from where he would get an almost uninterrupted 'line of sight' into Cwm-y-Llan and beyond into Cwm Tregalan.

Both this area and that between the Rhyd-Ddu road and South Ridge of Snowdon were being searched by dogs, followed up by 'line-searching' groups. Notwithstanding the limitations of human searchers at night, the four missing boys had to be in one or other of these main search areas, and, in view of the circumstances of the incident, it was considered a reasonable bet that if the dogs did not find them, one of the follow-up groups might be lucky enough to stumble across them.

By midnight the weather had begun to improve and the wind dropped to little more than a gentle breeze. Over in Cwm-y-Llan, as I worked Gwynne up the slope, criss-crossing the valley, I could see at least three dog handlers' lights slowly descending the almost precipitous side of South Ridge into Cwm Tregalan. The dogs had given strong indications up on the ridge, and the handlers were convinced that they were on to a find as it would have been easy for the exhausted Scouts to have been blown off the path and over the edge. In fact the dogs were picking up the scent of items of equipment which the Scouts had jettisoned, and which had been blown across the ridge and had then rolled down the slope. The dogs found several pieces of gear which led the handlers to believe that the Scouts themselves were further down into the cwm.

None of the Scouts was found however and, as the dogs had completed the search of their given area, they were withdrawn at 4.00 a.m. and returned to the search base in Rhyd-Ddu to rest until daylight. As the other search groups completed their tasks, they also returned to base, and it was planned

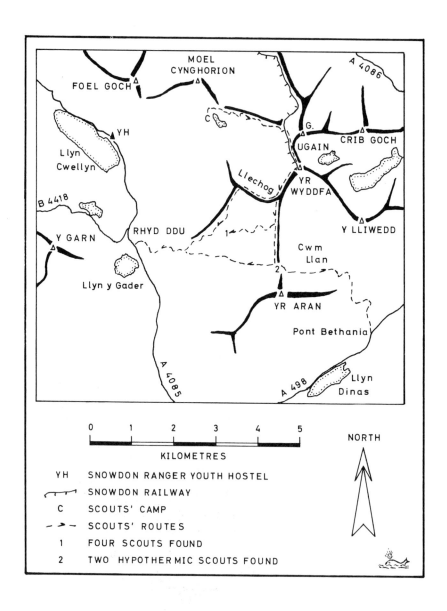

FOEL GOCH

MOEL CYNGHORION

A 4086

YH

Llyn Cwellyn

C

G.
UGAIN

CRIB GOCH

B 4418

Llechog

YR WYDDFA

Y GARN

RHYD DDU

1

Y LLIWEDD

Cwm Llan

Llyn y Gader

2

YR ARAN

Pont Bethania

A 4085

A 498

Llyn Dinas

0   1   2   3   4   5

KILOMETRES

NORTH

YH   SNOWDON RANGER YOUTH HOSTEL

SNOWDON RAILWAY

C   SCOUTS' CAMP

SCOUTS' ROUTES

1   FOUR SCOUTS FOUND

2   TWO HYPOTHERMIC SCOUTS FOUND

to restart the search soon after first light, bringing in more fresh searchers. The Rescue Co-ordination Centre at Pitreavie made the three helicopters of C flight available, and they began over-flying the area as soon as it was light enough to see. At about 9.00 a.m. one of the helicopters spotted a small, bright blue tent tucked away almost out of sight in the angle of two mountain walls. In fact they had already flown over the tent twice without seeing it, and the third time the four boys came out of their tent and waved yellow bivvy bags. They were cold but reasonably well considering the experience they had been through and were flown to Bangor hospital for a check-up. After treatment for cold-exhaustion they were discharged to rejoin their demoralised colleagues.

The action of the four boys was the one bright spot in this otherwise disastrous catalogue of errors. Apparently deserted by their adult leader, and then separated from the most experienced member of their group – the Venture Scout who had died from hypothermia – these four young lads had the sense to get themselves down to lower ground and pitch their tent in the most sheltered place they could find. They had worked their way down through the broken, rocky terrain of Cwm Garegog and were found much further down the mountain than anyone expected, and well below the areas which had been searched by either the search dogs or other groups. It is worth recording that these lads had been trained personally by the expedition leader, and but for that, and had they not used their common sense and initiative in seeking shelter, they could easily have become hypothermic and died.

Although the expedition leader said, "It was a properly organised expedition and we had been arranging for months where we were going to stop," clearly the detailed planning fell short of the standards laid down by the Scout Association itself. The leader appeared to have little understanding of what gale force winds are like high up in the mountains, and perhaps more emphasis should be put on training leaders in the precise meaning of various Met office terms. To this end I have included the chapter 'Weather Warning' at the beginning of this book.

In British mountains bad weather is normal; good weather is a bonus. But any one venturing onto the hills must understand how severe the weather can be and how quickly and often dramatically it can change. To recap, in this incident the leader said, "We couldn't have expected such a dramatic change in the weather" and his belief that it would get better might have been why no escape routes were used if indeed they had been planned. But if, as he said, they had been preparing the expedition for so long beforehand, this argument would not hold, as one of the essential factors in their plan should have been what to do if things went wrong. Escape routes must be included in any route, regardless of what the weather might do. An accident or sudden illness is just as likely to make it necessary to get down to lower levels quickly in good weather as in bad.

If faced with a problem a leader must consider all the facts at his disposal and then make a calculated decision. In this incident the leader, who was responsible for thirty-seven people, was suddenly faced with conditions beyond his experience and he based his decision purely on his assumption that the weather would get better. He also stated that he had made the wrong assumption that the snow would be coming in from the north which resulted in his decision to lead his party due south into the full force of the storm, all of which suggests that he was less experienced than he should have been to lead such a large group of youngsters. The planning of an expedition, especially in mountainous country, must always take into consideration the possibility, even the probability, that something may go wrong. To decide on a route without any thought of alternative plans and to carry out the plan, come what may, is to invite disaster.

And what of the other adults in the party? In one national newspaper the leader was reported as saying, "The Scouts had good leaders, with an adult in charge of each group." Yet one of those leaders told the Press, "I haven't been up Snowdon before and I don't want to go again. I didn't think I would make it down." He was in charge of the group which lost the two boys who were found by the lady walker on Bwlch-y-Llan and the four who found their own way down and who were located by the helicopter next morning. So where was he? Was this good leadership to leave six young boys to fend for themselves? As Park warden Sam Roberts, who has since become a veteran of two major Everest expeditions, said at the time, "The boys had good equipment, but it is experience that matters when one is tired and hypothermic. The mountains are made for adventure, but the leaders in charge of these groups have been irresponsible in taking them out, and in their supervision they have failed badly."

Amongst the many stories about the incident in local and national newspapers, I read the following quotation by the warden of a centre to which some of the Scouts who made their way down to the road were taken, 'They assembled at the top (Snowdon summit) and made the right decision to take the most direct descent to safety.' **Wrong!** In navigation the most direct route is not necessarily the quickest or easiest; in fact it is seldom so, and again we come back to escape routes which should be pre-planned so that in cases of difficulty you know at once which is the best way down. It could never have been the right decision to struggle on into the teeth of the gale just because it happened to be the direct route down to their destination. The object in such dreadful conditions is survival and you should always use your pre-planned safe way off, even if it means ending up in the next valley, or back where you started from. However inconvenient it may be to have to organise your party and get them to their original destination, at least you will have brought them all safely down. Better to lose a bit of face than to have to attend a coroner's inquest.

If he had done his homework properly, the leader would have led the party from the summit down the railway line to Bwlch Glas, then down The Zigzags and Miners Track to Pen-y-Pass Youth Hostel. Once off the ridge descending The Zigzags, they would have been protected from the full blast of the storm by the high ridges to the south but, above all, at no time would they have been committed to walking directly into the gale. And they would all have survived.

As a result of this incident, The Scout Association conducted a wide ranging review of its operating practices with regard to all activities on Moors, Hills and Mountains. The review resulted in a number of changes to both the Rules and operating procedures of the Association which are:–

That a more positive system of authorisation of leaders of expeditions should be introduced nationally.

That there should be a compulsory session on activity safety on all Scout Leader Basic Training Courses.

That an official Route plan form be produced and made available by the Association.

That every party must complete two copies of this Route Plan – one to be carried by the party, and the other to be left with a responsible person.

That every party must carry an official Emergency Card which would be made available through the Association's headquarters.

All these changes were implemented within a very short time after the review.

Incidents of this kind bring leaders and others involved into contact with the media whose job it is to 'get a good story'. It is perhaps an opportune moment to sound a warning to be extremely careful what you actually say to them. I find it hard to believe that the warden of an outdoor activity centre or a youth hostel would have said what he was reported as saying about taking the most direct route down. It is so easy to be misquoted, and with hindsight he must have realised what a stupid remark it appeared to be. Then again be guarded against the catch question. In the incident described in chapter 13, after reaching the road at midnight, the leader was questioned by the Press and explained why he had decided to bring the team off the hill without the body. A final question caught him off-guard – "and what are you going to do now?" "Me? I'm going home to a nice warm bed," he said. "But that's not for publication," he added, as he realised how this might appear in the headlines. 'Rescuer leaves casualty on hill as he goes home to bed' or something equally sinister, he thought. It was too late; the national tabloid concerned headlined his remark and slated him, which was pretty shabby treatment for a man who had spent five hours on the mountain in atrocious conditions trying to get the body down, for no reward other than the inner satisfaction all MR people feel when they go out to rescue, or recover, one of their own. Journalists do not see it in the same light; they have a living to earn, and anything which might make a good story is fair game. So the lesson we should all learn from this is to be very cautious and think carefully before saying anything at all to anyone. Not all that easy when you are tired and dispirited!

On a bleak November day in the early 1970s a party of school children under the leadership of two young adults set out to cross the Cairngorm plateau. As might have been expected at that time of year blizzards had been forecast, but although the leaders had been urged by local mountaineers and ski instructors at White Lady Shieling not to attempt the expedition, they persisted in keeping to their planned programme. Even when the ski lifts closed because of the fast-deteriorating weather they did not see the danger; furthermore they split the party into two groups, the older and more experienced male leader taking the stronger children, leaving the girl leader, who was barely out of her teens, to cope with the younger and less robust age group.

Up on the plateau, as the blizzard developed the older group struggled on, spending the night in the high-level Curran bothy, which has since been demolished. The following day, they descended the March Burn into the Lairig Ghru – a three-hundred-metre-deep ravine which cuts right through the Cairngorms from north to south. Meantime the younger group, walking into the teeth of the gale across the blizzard-swept and featureless plateau, was soon in deep trouble. Battling against the gale, almost suffocated by the driven snow, the children soon became exhausted and it was obvious to the leader that she must try to build some sort of shelter and save what strength they had left. But as quickly as she piled up a bank of snow for protection, it was flattened by the wind. She was in a desperate, nightmarish situation and whilst she did all she possibly could to save her charges, they collapsed and died one after the other. When the rescue team found them two days later, no fewer than five children had lost their lives.

In her book "Two Star Red", about the RAF Mountain Rescue Teams and published in 1964, Gwen Moffat wrote – 'splitting the party has been the cause of many accidents . . . it's a principle of mountaineering that a party should never be split except in an emergency. (After an accident someone has to go for help and if there are more than two people in the party, at least one of them must stay with the injured person. If there are only two people in the group, the casualty must be left.)

Despite this rule people continue to split the party, deliberately and voluntarily – and even in poor weather conditions.' Prophetic writing, for this is exactly what happened in this Cairngorm tragedy. Seemingly nothing changes, but leaders should take note and learn from other people's mistakes.

Sometimes bad leadership, by adults who send their charges into wild and remote places, brings out unseen qualities in some of the youngsters who find themselves lost or in difficulties, as happened in the story of the Scouts on 'The Killer Mountain'. In this context I am referring to leaders who send parties out on ill-prepared expeditions with inadequate instructions about what to do in case of accident or illness, when to abort the exercise, what to do if they miss check points, fall behind schedule, and so on. One such incident occurred in July 1985 when a party of Scouts from the London area was lost and stranded overnight on the northern part of the Moelwyns above Nantmor, not far from Beddgelert. It was a really filthy night with torrential rain falling until dawn, and the hills were awash. Five dog teams were called out and were briefed by a member of the Aberglaslyn Hall centre where the Scouts were staying (the staff of the centre were not involved in the exercise in any way), and were deployed by 2.00 a.m. This area is one of the roughest and wildest in Snowdonia. There are few footpaths, and because of the bad visibility the Scouts had been following a cross-country route on compass bearings.

It was heavy going for the SARDA teams and required a lot of care negotiating the wet, broken ground and slippery rocks. At about 5.30 a.m. search dog Jet with Phil Benbow (he always seemed to pick the lucky straw) picked up a scent blowing across a lake and followed it to a ridge about three hundred metres below the summit of Cnicht – the Snowdon Matterhorn – immediately above where the Scouts were sheltering against a rock wall in their sleeping bags and tents. The boys were all safe and well considering the conditions, though they were very cold, tired and hungry. They were led off the hill to the nearest road-head where transport had been sent round for them. They looked a sorry sight and it was at once obvious that some of the lads were inadequately equipped for an expedition of this sort, in that they were wearing 'trainers' and jeans, both of which were totally unsuitable for the terrain and weather.

As the Scouts told their story back in the centre, we learned that there were seven of them altogether, their ages ranging from eleven to fifteen. They were poorly equipped generally for what they had set out to do, and we were all very critical that such young and inexperienced boys should be let loose on the mountain without any adult supervision. The Scoutmasters had arranged to rendezvous with the group at their camp-site in the evening, but this had not happened. The severe weather was unexpected in the middle of July and once again no one had bothered to listen to a weather forecast. If they had, they must have turned a deaf ear, and it highlights once again the fact that the weather is just as likely to turn 'atrocious' in July as in January.

As the day had progressed, the Scouts began to fall behind schedule. Two of them had become so tired that they discarded their rucksacks with all their survival gear and food at the bottom of a waterfall where they were eventually found and recovered. They had been given no fixed route and were expected to find their way cross-country to the appointed camp-site. The wild, rough terrain proved too much for them and they failed to find it, and they finally decided to shelter for the night where we found them next morning.

The 'hero of the hour' was the fifteen-year-old leader who had been given explicit instructions to meet their Scoutmaster at the rendezvous, with no alternative. I think this irresponsible and unfair order should never have been given, but it was just another example of a failing amongst adult leaders which is far too common. It denies young leaders the chance of using their initiative and common sense, and much of the value of such expeditions, which is to develop initiative and leadership qualities, is lost. This boy therefore pressed on into the wilderness when logically he knew he should have given it best and turned back, thus avoiding the traumatic experience of the party getting lost. Had the Scout party been allowed alternatives, it would have saved all the SARDA teams the inconvenience and risk involved in spending much of the night out on the mountain in such appalling weather. It took two and a half hours to walk the Scouts down to the road which is an indication of how difficult the terrain was.

It seems unfortunate that in this chapter I have included three examples of poor leadership which involved Scout groups, and readers may get the impression that the standards within the Scout movement are inadequate. This is not so, and it must be said that they have a very strict code of conduct for their leaders which demands the same high standards as The Mountain-walking Leader Training Board. This is borne out by the action taken by the Scout Association immediately after the tragic incident on Snowdon.

There is only a very thin line between adventure and foolhardiness, a fact which can sometimes be overlooked by the 'parent body' whether it be a school or other organisation. In a serious incident, especially one resulting in the death of, or serious injury to, youngsters, there is always an immediate reaction to whitewash publicly the expedition leader. In some cases, after the initial whitewash, and no doubt after more mature consideration, very severe disciplinary action has been taken against leaders who have been shown to have been foolhardy, but in order to protect the parent body in the event of legal action being taken against them, it is kept very much under wraps. How much more sensible it would be to cut out the whitewash and if there has been a mistake, admit it. It might hurt a bit, but at least others could learn from what happened.

Referring back to the number of Scout groups being involved in outdoor activity incidents, it must be realised that far more Scout groups carry out expeditions and other such activities than groups from any other organisation. By the law of averages, therefore, they will feature more frequently in accident statistics. The Scout Association does everything possible to ensure that their boys are properly led, but it is not possible to exercise control once a group is committed to an expedition and is out on its own. And if a leader is found to have acted irresponsibly and to have endangered his group by departing from the guide-lines, the Scout movement is unforgiving.

To make a change from stories about the Scouts, the next incident is one which involved Army cadets led by a captain. It happened after a few days of relatively warm, fine weather during the early Spring in 1989. On the day in question there was a sudden change to bitterly cold conditions as the wind swung round to the north-east and fronts swept across the country from Scandinavia. High up there was sleet and snow with sub-zero temperatures which, in the strong winds, produced a severe wind-chill effect.

The party of cadets was walking up the Watkin Path to the summit of Snowdon and at the western end of Bwlch-y-Saethau, just before the final ascent, a fifteen-year-old cadet collapsed with cold-exhaustion. The captain quite correctly put him in a bivvy-bag in the shelter of some rocks beside the path, as he judged that there was a serious risk of the boy becoming hypothermic. And that was the only thing he did right during the whole incident. There happened to be two other walkers there at the time and it seems that the captain asked them to stay with the casualty whilst he went for help. Instead of going down to Nant Gwynant, which was clearly the shortest and quickest route to a telephone, he led the whole of the rest of his party to the summit leaving the sick cadet with two complete strangers. Any responsible leader would have put the well-being of his boys before the completion of the planned expedition. However disappointing it may be to have to turn back, if the life of one member of the group is at risk, the decision to do so must be made. On arrival at the summit, the captain and his cadets spent about an hour breaking into one of the station out-buildings, which turned out to be the station-master's office, to try to get some shelter. But by this time the captain himself was suffering from the first signs of hypothermia and he took no further part in the proceedings. He lay inside the building, cold, wet and exhausted.

By now garbled messages were beginning to reach the wardens' centre at Pen-y-Pass but it was quite a long time before it became clear that there were in fact two hypothermia cases. The wardens, assisted by members of the Llanberis MRT, eventually evacuated the captain down the railway line to a position below cloud base where a helicopter from C flight picked him up and flew him down to the valley. The cadet was then located and again the helicopter airlifted him off the mountain. When the captain was found in the building, he was still wearing his saturated clothes but in his rucksack there was a complete set of dry clothing. Either he had not the initiative to change into them, or the degree of hypothermia had passed the stage at which the victim is able to help himself. The incident was an appalling example of bad leadership. When the cadet collapsed it should have been a warning to an alert leader that they should turn back. Ambition to reach the summit took over, the warning was ignored, the leader himself succumbed to the cold, and the whole expedition became an utter shambles. Any responsible leader of youngsters should always feel that his duty is to the parents of the boys committed to his charge and in no circumstances should any of them be left alone on the hillside, even if some strangers offer to stay with him. It must be right for the strangers to go down to get help; the leader's duty is to stay with his charges. In this incident the boy was sick and needed reassurance, and to see all his mates pushing on without him was a pretty extraordinary way of giving it.

The Right to Risk one's Life

I have often wondered what makes a minority of mountaineers so resolutely opposed to telling someone where they are going before they set out to walk or climb in the hills. Is it sheer laziness, or is it the 'macho' instinct, more common amongst rock-climbers than walkers, that 'I'm indestructible; it will never happen to me'? It may not be either of these, but rather a deeply-felt resentment against being asked to conform, which some people regard as an unwarranted attack on their freedom to do as they please.

Of course, it's no such thing. Walkers and climbers alike are asked to leave word with a responsible person so that if they do not return from their expedition by the time they have indicated, the local rescue services can respond and begin planning the necessary action. The really important thing is that they will know where to start looking for missing people. It makes it very much more difficult when there is no route-card at all, or when people change their minds – as happened on Snowdon at the end of January 1990. A party of twelve Scouts were on the summit when heavy snow began to fall, reducing visibility to almost nil. Instead of aborting their walk and using their planned escape route down the Miners Track, the leader decided it would be easier to follow the Watkin Path and then climb over Lliwedd before descending to the Miners Track at the eastern end of Llyn Llydaw. They lost their way in the white-out, blundered on to Gallt-y-Wenallt and then down into the Gwynant valley. When they failed to turn up at their estimated time, a search party with dogs, acting on the information given on their route-card, set out soon after dark to cover the Miners Track. Of course, there was no sign of the Scouts, who were eventually found safe and well some hours later. Sometimes circumstances may dictate that a planned route has to be changed, but in this case the thinking behind the decision to ignore the obvious escape route is difficult to understand. I can think of no circumstances in which failure to prepare a route-card at all can possibly be excused, as the following story shows.

Two men had booked into our hotel in Llanberis. One, a big chap standing well over six feet, quickly let everyone know that he was an experienced rock-climber. His companion, a much smaller man, had never been on the mountains before and he had been brought to Snowdonia to be initiated into hill-walking by the 'expert'. At the bar the big man did all the talking and you could almost hear his 'ironmongery' clanking every time he raised his beer mug. His companion and the other guests were politely impressed – or were they? Before they went out next morning I asked them where they were going, and whether they would be back for dinner. They said they were intending to walk over the Carneddau and would definitely be in for dinner, at about 6.00 p.m. I gave them a blank route-card to fill in, but it was ignored. They did not arrive back at the hotel until 10.15 p.m., by which time I had informed Tony Jones at 'Oggie' and had asked the police to have all the parking places round the Carneddau massif checked. Their car was nowhere to be seen, and we assumed that they were no longer in the area and that there would be no point in starting a 'needle in a haystack' search until we had some clues as to where they might be.

After finishing their walk on the Carneddau the two men had gone to a hotel in Capel Curig for dinner and then spent an hour or two drinking without letting anyone know, which was particularly thoughtless. When the 'big man' was told that the police had been looking for his car, he became very aggressive and demanded to know by what right we had asked them to help. I pointed out that we had only started routine procedures, and that as we had not found their car we had decided to take no further action until we had something to go on. I also told him that if he had been lying out there with a sprained ankle he would have been the first to shout "where the hell's the bloody rescue team?" He refused to accept that they had done anything wrong, seemed quite unable to see the other point of view, and as soon as he had finished his beer he went off to bed. A night's sleep failed to calm his anger and after breakfast he checked out. We, along with the other guests, were glad to see him go!

As he left, he swore that as a matter of principle he would never, ever, fill in a route-card, and of course he was perfectly within his rights to take that attitude. His companion, however, was a much less arrogant and aggressive person and he saw our side of the argument. He quietly apologised for his friend's boorish behaviour and slipped a 'fiver' into the SARDA collecting box.

In February 1987 a lone climber, 26-year-old John Carter, fell and injured himself. The story of his accident and how he was eventually found and brought to safety is told in detail in chapter 24 – 'Moral Fibre and Self Rescue'. However, the fact is that he went out on his own without telling anyone where he was going, what he was intending to do, or what time he would return. It was sheer good luck that a French student staying in the youth hostel had in fact spotted John making his way across to the Trinity Gullies on Clogwyn-y-Garnedd on Snowdon.

There have been many incidents over the years when individuals or groups staying in hostels or hotels have gone out without leaving a route-card. When they do not turn up for their evening meal, their absence is noticed by the staff and other residents. Sometimes, as in John's case, they have been seen on the hill, but very often there is no clue as to their possible whereabouts and that presents a big problem for the searchers – where do they start looking? Also when people staying in their own huts or tents go out without telling anyone, incidents which, with help from a MRT usually end happily, can easily turn into disasters. If these people are unlucky enough to have an accident, become ill, or get stuck for any reason, it is not simply a case of 'the Rescue' not knowing where to start looking for them, for no one even knows they have gone out, or when they expected to be back, so no-one is concerned for their safety.

In early November 1982, a party of six students from Oxford polytechnic, who were staying in a club hut in the Ogwen valley, went to climb on the Idwal Slabs. This was not a remote area and was little more than a kilometre from Ogwen Cottage on the A5 road. This may have influenced them not to bother leaving word at the cottage, but it was a flawed decision. It was 1.30 p.m. when they started their climb and as they would have had to return to the road for their vehicle, it would not have been out of their way to leave a route-card at the cottage on the way out to the Slabs.

The group was under the leadership of Randolph Taylor, President of the Polytechnic Mountaineering Club, but between them they did not have very much experience. They reached the top of the route in the dark, but all of their torches had been left at the foot of the crag as they did not anticipate that it would take them so long. Due to their unfamiliarity with the area and being unable to see their surroundings, they could not find the 'walk off' and Taylor decided they would have to abseil down. Ropes were prepared for the descent and four of the group, including Taylor and nineteen-year-old Archie Cameron, reached a ledge 25 metres below. They could find no suitable belays to continue the descent and they therefore tied a second rope to a loop in the first which would give them enough length to reach the ground. Cameron volunteered to go first and Taylor explained exactly what he had to do. He started to go down, immediately disappearing out of view of the others, and almost at once his colleagues heard a scream followed by a thud. He had obviously fallen and they called to him but heard no response

Llyn Idwal and the Slabs (left), Nameless Cwm and the upper cliff of Glyder Fawr (top left).   *Tony Welch*

other than groaning for a few moments, then silence.

Taylor then tried to find a way down to where Cameron was believed to be lying, but found himself stuck on an overhanging rock and could neither go down, as he'd come to the end of the rope, nor could he climb back up because the rock was wet and slippery. He tried to get his friends to lower another rope to him but although they could hear him shouting, they couldn't understand what he was telling them to do. There was nothing more he could do until daylight, and the whole party had to stay where they were, hanging on to the rock face for the rest of the night. It was not until about 9.30 a.m. that two climbers heard their shouts and raised the alarm.

The 'Oggie' team was called out and got them all off the crag, together with Archie Cameron's body, and took them down to the road.

A team spokesman told the Press, "No one knew they were there because they hadn't bothered to tell anyone where they were going . . . " which is the whole point of the story. If they **had** left word with somebody, when they failed to return on time , he would have alerted the police, and the rescue team would have gone out to look for them straight away, i.e. at about 8.00 p.m., and got them all safely down some fifteen hours earlier – perhaps even before Archie Cameron fell. It is a matter of discipline to remember that if you have left a route-card you **must** report the safe return of your party immediately you get off the hill. All too often, in the euphoria of having done a good route, people forget that they have asked someone to watch out for them and go off for a drink or a meal without reporting in. They are then probably safely ensconced in a pub or a café whilst the rescue services are already out looking for them. On one occasion, after having a meal and a few drinks, the 'missing' people actually, though unwittingly, joined in the search for themselves!

In any out-door activity there must be an element of hazardous adventure, and therein lies a basic conflict between a minority who cherish their freedom to 'risk it all', and the commitment of society in general, but kindred spirits in particular, to rescue a fellow human being who is thought to be in difficulty. Those in the minority group would like to be free of any obligation to other out-door activists who feel it's their duty to rescue someone in trouble. Both points of view are understandable and natural. The minority demand their legitimate freedom to push themselves to their physical limits, and to strive to achieve ever more difficult goals. That is their right and we can but wonder where we would be if our forbears had never taken risks – if Columbus had never set out or astronauts had not left the ground to land on the Moon. It is a natural, inborn urge in mankind which cannot be suppressed and has to be fulfilled. On the other hand, rescue and recovery is a human instinct as well, and there is nothing more satisfying or worthy than to put one's own life on the line to rescue someone else, whether he be a friend or a complete stranger. To take part in a rescue operation is an exhilarating experience, and very considerable risks and material costs are often involved to fulfil the need to save life or recover bodies. I include the latter because the law of the land, no less than our morality, demands that bodies must be brought back and given a proper, dignified disposal.

That section of society which does not approve of, or take part in, hazardous out-door activities, criticises those who do and tries to limit the risk-taking. 'Make them pay,' goes up the cry whenever there has been a particularly dramatic rescue which has hit the headlines. But it's not that easy to implement, although in many countries rescues are charged for. In some places, too, there are restrictive regulations, but they are almost always considered by participants to be unacceptable and unenforceable, and if a mountaineer wants to risk his life through being too ambitious, and lacking experience and adequate equipment, it's his right to do so.

Notwithstanding foolishness or irresponsibility on the part of mountaineers or other out-door activists, their peers still have the sacrosanct duty to go to their aid if they get into difficulties, and rescue teams throughout Britain, whether they be civilian, Services, coastguard, police or ad hoc groups of eager volunteers, will answer a call for help at any time. I do not believe there has ever been, nor can there be, an incident in this country to compare with that on the Eiger in Switzerland in the 1950s when the local guides said the North Face was too dangerous, and if anyone attempted to climb it and got into trouble, they would not try to rescue them. When two Italians ignored the warning and became storm-bound a thousand feet below the summit, it was obvious they would need help. But the majority of the local guides steadfastly refused to go out, and in no time climbers from all over Europe rushed to help the crag-fast Italians. They managed to haul one of them to the top, but despite desperate efforts they could not reach the other man who had roped himself to a piton. He eventually died, his body slipped off the ledge, and for years it dangled at the end of his rope as a ghastly warning for all to see – and an embarrassment to the guides who had refused to help.

When conditions are thought to be too dangerous in Britain, authorities such as the National Parks warden or ranger services, the police, and sometimes MRT leaders, send out clear warnings through the media. Some misguided adventurers do ignore the advice given, but the wardens, police and rescue teams have never yet shirked their duty. There can be no restrictive legislation dividing 'the sheep from the goats,' the experienced mountaineer from the novice. Not only would this be manifestly unfair, but if novices were to be denied the opportunity to go out and learn in hazardous conditions, there would soon be no experienced mountaineers left. A novice should always seek the help and advice of more experienced people before going out in such conditions. Far too often they hear the warnings on the media, and rush up to the mountains to take advantage of 'Alpine' snow and ice with little or no knowledge of how to use crampons or an ice-axe. Then, rather than trying out techniques at low levels, they get as high as they can, and wonder why there are so many accidents.

The right of an out-door activist to take risks is valid as long as he does not directly endanger anyone else. On the other hand rescuers must have the right to refuse to attempt a rescue in exceptionally bad conditions. This right will very rarely be invoked, but it should be appreciated that MRT leaders bear a very heavy responsibility to their members, no less than to the person they are trying to rescue. They may sometimes have a very difficult decision to make concerning whether to attempt to rescue or whether, in view of deteriorating conditions and serious risk to the lives of their fellow members, to abort an operation on which they have already embarked. No hard and fast rules can be laid down, but the overriding principle must be that the rescuers should never become the rescued.

Any responsible person will appreciate that his risk-taking activity may well put someone else's life in danger, and the only way he can overcome this unpalatable conclusion is to go off to climb in a remote area without telling anyone where he is going! The commitment of our rescue services is such, however, that as soon as the risk-taker's absence is noticed, no effort will be spared to find him and bring him safely back. Perhaps in this way honour is satisfied on both sides.

The human body can be likened to a ship. When the vessel is tied up in harbour it is safe, but that is not what it was built for. So the human body should not be wrapped in cotton wool and kept indoors. We should follow our natural instinct and go out and strive, but aspiring mountaineers should get all the experience they can, and by taking care, preparing properly, and always acting in a responsible way, they will stand a much better chance of surviving to enjoy the mountains for very many years. Remember – it's your right to die if you must, but it's not your right to take someone else with you.

"Hard Men, too, have Emotions"

You are called to the telephone and told there is an incident on. Whatever you are told, the adrenalin starts pumping and you begin to wonder what horror you will be faced with out there on the mountain. I have met very few members of MRTs who try to appear 'super-macho'. Even those who are by nature less sensitive to traumatic experiences than most, have deep-seated emotions. The 'macho-man' is a product of society, not of nature, and he finds no place amongst the ranks of the genuine MR fraternity. In fact quite the obverse is true and most of those involved possess a masculinity in which tenderness plays a major part. When tragedies unfold before them, they are as emotional as everyone else, but their acquired veneer prevents it showing and they tend to give the impression that they are not affected.

Members of MRTs are not trained to deal with the traumas of death or shattered bodies, nor with the grief of friends and relations. It is something they either come to terms with, or cannot accept and pack it in. During my early days in MR, I often asked myself why on earth I was doing it. My Welsh blood makes me a very emotional person but my Army days in Burma and Korea had inured me to the worst horrors of death and injury – even to the thankless job of writing to the wives and mothers of the casualties. However, nothing can prepare one for the emotional trauma of breaking the devastating news face to face with someone on the mountain.

One early call-out caused me to seriously consider whether MR was for me and, in retrospect, I wonder if I had really thought it through. When I got the call, the excitement was intense and I dashed off to the MRT base to see what it was all about. A 29-year-old climber was lying seriously injured at the foot of a crag about five hundred metres from Dinas Mot towards Pen-y-Pass. Apparently he and his father had been climbing together the previous day, but the weather had suddenly deteriorated, thick cloud came down, and they had left some of the gear at the top of the crag. Next morning the younger man had climbed up to recover it, but his father had decided to give it a miss; he was a man of around 60 years of age, and he waited at the foot of the climb. Having retrieved the equipment, the son started to abseil down, but almost at once his belay slipped off and he plummeted to the bottom, landing face down across a large boulder, and right at the feet of his father. He was clearly in a bad way, and his father raced down to the road to raise the alarm.

When the rescue team arrived, the casualty was still conscious, but having great difficulty breathing. A quick examination showed that he had crushed his rib cage, and there was nothing we could do except to carry him to the road where an ambulance was already waiting. As we started down, I looked at the older man's face. He obviously knew that his son was dying, and our eyes met. As a father myself, I read the utter desolation the man was feeling, and I felt his own despair to the pit of my stomach. It all seemed unreal and not, somehow, what I had expected to see.

Other team members were obviously feeling the same sort of emotion, but, as we carried the dying man down the steep slope as gently and carefully as we could, their reactions seemed curious and almost objectionable to me. Later, with more experience, I came to realise that their false cheerfulness and joking as a man lay dying on the stretcher, was the only way they could hide their sadness and get on with the job. On several incidents when a rescue had become a recovery, this 'trying to be dispassionate' syndrome was there, and in one incident it so upset a team member, whose religion demanded the utmost respect for the dead, that a complaint about undue ribaldry was made and the team was asked to tone their levity down and show more deference.

The shock of suddenly coming face to face with death, perhaps on a lovely sunny day in the most beautiful surroundings you could imagine, is something you have got to be prepared for. Every incident presents the same problems in this respect, but eventually I did come to terms with it all and it no longer bothered me at the time. It is the after-effects which are probably more upsetting, such as having to tell a close friend or relative of the casualty, what has happened, or dealing with extremely emotional members of the casualty's party. I well remember one occasion when a colleague of mine – a very tough character – was involved in a heart-attack incident high up on Snowdon. A Scout-master collapsed soon after having his lunch, and his fourteen-year-old son was with him when he died. The boy was very stoical but what my friend found almost too upsetting was the bravery of the young boy in coping with the unintentionally cruel chatter of his friends. They just did not know how to react to such a tragedy.

Pent-up emotions must eventually find a way out, and an incident which occurred in the Ogwen Valley several years ago well illustrates this. SARDA had been exercising in Cwm Eigiau, but radio signals about a serious incident on Tryfan were coming through loud and clear. As we had finished the day's programme, we all jumped into our vehicles and drove round to 'Oggie' base to see if we could be of any assistance. There were two casualties half-way up the North Ridge and a large number of stretcher-bearers were needed – it was going to be a long and difficult carry-off with frequent changes of carrying parties. By the time we reached the casualties (both teenage boys who had been blown off the ridge by a violent gust of wind), one of them was already dead from severe head injuries and the other was in a very bad way. The first priority was to get the injured boy down to the waiting ambulance as quickly as possible, and the carrying parties involved were aware that they were in a race against time.

When they came off the hill they were hindered by a television camera-man who was hell-bent on getting a good picture. He got in the way and was very roughly thrown across the path by some of the rescuers, and measured his length at the bottom of a bank. His camera was damaged and, over the next few days, there followed bitter recrimination between the camera-man, who after all had been trying to earn his living, and those who regarded him as a 'bloody nuisance'. Of course there are two sides to the argument, and whilst to some extent I was sorry for the man being manhandled and his valuable equipment damaged, on the other hand I was one of the stretcher-bearers who were impeded by him. We were doing all we could to save the boy's life and the camera-man should have realised this: it seems that his selfish and insensitive behaviour got its just deserts. I am sure that in less fraught circumstances he would have been asked to move and no doubt he would have done so. But it was a measure of how emotional rescuers sometimes become that their feelings got the better of them and they resorted to violence.

On prolonged searches, such as that for the young girl, Anna Humphries, on the borders of Clwyd and Shropshire, which lasted for a whole week in November 1988, you begin to know you are not going to find the missing person alive. The enjoyment of working your dog gradually disappears and, although you want to go on and make a find, it becomes progressively over-shadowed by the increasing certainty that you are too late. Inevitably you wonder whether you have perhaps missed the casualty, and the nagging doubt takes a long time to go. The same doubts appear on rescues when, in spite of all your efforts to save a seriously injured person, he does not survive. You invariably punish yourself by wondering whether, if you had done something differently, or had been quicker, you might have kept him alive.

Some of the incidents the rescue services are called out to deal with can be very traumatic. The Lockerbie disaster was probably the worst possible scenario for rescuers, partly because of the horrific sights they were faced with, and partly because of the huge number of people whose shattered bodies were scattered over the countryside. It was Christmas 1988 and, when SARDA was asked to help, many handlers left their families in the middle of their Christmas dinners, and set off for Lockerbie. Every one of our handlers in Wales was involved at one time or another, and each one had distressing stories to tell. It was all so different from anything any of them had ever expected to have to cope with, and it took most of them many weeks to get over this harrowing experience. Of the forty-seven handlers who took part in the Lockerbie search, no fewer than five eventually suffered from post-trauma shock. This is a condition brought about by some distressing incident such as a massive railway accident or a Lockerbie-type disaster, and it seems that those most susceptible are people who have no-one with whom to talk about their experience. It all gets bottled up and eventually manifests itself as a feeling of inadequacy or guilt. "Why all of them and not me?" seems to be the notion which in turn produces a persecution complex. The five cases resulting from Lockerbie have all resigned from SARDA as they could no longer face going out into the unknown.

"A Question of Values"

The high tops of Snowdonia were coated with a thin layer of frozen snow, making the going slippery and dangerous for the unwary. I had almost reached the summit cairn when I saw a lone figure poised on the edge of the precipitous east face of Snowdon – Clogwyn-y-Garnedd. Mindful of the ice underfoot, I made my way carefully down the spur towards him, noticing as I went a young lad sheltering behind the rocks.

"Hullo," I said, as I approached the man. "You're not thinking of jumping, are you?" I asked, not sure whether that was the right approach. "No, I'm not," he replied. "My boy – that's him sitting up there – dropped his glove down here and I want to get it back." He looked round at me and added, "You've got an ice-axe; give me a lend of it, will you?" "No way," I replied as I peered cautiously over the edge to see the glove lying 10 metres or so below. "You must be mad to think of going down there. How much climbing have you done?" The dialogue which followed left me in no doubt that he was not a climber, had no experience of winter mountaineering and was only a casual summer hill-walker at best. "Well," I went on, "my advice to you is to forget the glove and get yourself and the boy safely down; he looks chilled to the marrow already. You can buy another pair of gloves in the village." "No," he retorted quite angrily, "my wife knitted those gloves for the boy and she'll kill me if I don't take them home." "You'll kill yourself if you try," I said as I walked away. A few minutes later I saw him approach a group of walkers who had a rope, and clearly he was trying to persuade them to lower him over the edge. Like me, they refused.

Twenty minutes later I was standing at the top of The Zigzags in Bwlch Glas when the 'glove man' came striding down the railway line, his boy dragging his unwilling feet several metres behind. "Since none of you buggers will help me," he shouted, "I'm going down to Llanberis to buy a rope and I'll be back up to get the glove." I was speechless for a moment, not believing what I was hearing, and I just hoped that the cost of a rope would bring him to his senses. Maybe the price of a new pair of gloves would be more attractive to him. The next time I was on the summit, a couple of weeks later, I had a look down the slope but there was no sign of the glove. Whether he had in fact recovered it, or the winter gales had blown it away – a more likely answer – we'll never know. This is a true story and illustrates how people, who in their ordinary lives are clear-minded and sensible, seem to lose all sense of proportion and values when they venture into the mountains. How that man could have weighed the value of a pair of gloves against that of his own life, but more importantly against the grief, misery and hardship his needless death would have caused his family, I shall never understand.

The incident which took place on Crib Goch early in 1985 (chapter 14) gives another example of how people get their values all wrong when under stress. On a lighter note the following story, which is not set in a mountain environment, further emphasises that the effects of stress are not restricted to any single social stratum, and regardless of material wealth, or lack of it, it causes people in all walks of life to lose sight of true values. This story, about a damaged anorak, was told to me by one of the people involved.

A teenager had just left school, and had found a new interest in sailing. He joined the local Yacht Club and soon found a niche, crewing for one of the club members. His mother felt that he should be properly equipped and amongst other items she bought him an expensive anorak which cost her £150. Soon afterwards, the yacht he was crewing ran into heavy weather, was 'pooped' by a so-called freak wave and was overwhelmed. Fortunately they were close inshore and all the crew members except the boy, whom we'll call Tom, managed to scramble ashore to raise the alarm. Tom was swept some distance down current and ended up on some inaccessible rocks on which he clung until help arrived. The inshore lifeboat was soon on the scene and managed to get a rope across to Tom and haul him on board where they found that he had suffered injuries to his chest and legs. He was having trouble with his breathing and it was decided to ask the nearby air-station to send a SAR helicopter to pick him up and get him to hospital. Within a very few minutes the chopper was on site, winched Tom up from the pitching lifeboat and delivered him safely to the hospital.

When Tom's mother came to see him, after satisfying herself that he was not too badly injured and would soon recover, her attention turned to the anorak she had bought him, and to her horror she found that it had been torn; not beyond repair, but torn nevertheless. Forgetting that her son was lying in a hospital bed and was lucky to be alive, she upbraided him for being so careless!

Some days later the lifeboat station commander received an account for £150 – the cost of replacing the anorak. He was not amused, rather he was annoyed that there was not a word of thanks for rescuing Tom, and he returned the account to the irate lady suggesting that the damage to the anorak was probably caused when Tom was swept onto the rocks, or even when he was being winched into the helicopter. Knowing the air-station commander, he suggested to the lady that she should send her account to him – which she did. In due course she received the following reply:–

Dear Madam

We very much regret the damage done to your son's anorak during the recent operation by one of our helicopters to save his life, and we accept liability for the £150 you are claiming from us.

However, enclosed please find our own account for costs incurred in the rescue which amount to £5,000. May we suggest that you deduct your claim for £150 which we agree to pay you, and we will be pleased to receive your cheque for the balance at your earliest convenience.

Yours etc . . .

Having signed the letter the station commander hoped that the lesson would be obvious enough. It was, for nothing more was heard about it.

Whether a life is put in the balance against a glove, a rucksack, or an expensive anorak, let us keep a sense of proportion and think carefully – is it really worth the risk to your life? And what about the risk to the lives of the people who go out to pick up the pieces?

Amphitheatre Gully – Carneddau

In February 1983 a party of two schoolmasters and seven senior boys from University College School in London arrived in Snowdonia to practise snow and ice climbing in preparation for an expedition to the Himalayas in August the same year. They reached the Ogwen Valley on Thursday February 17th and left their vehicle parked at Gwern Gof Isaf. They then walked over to Cwm Eigiau and set up base camp under Craig-yr-Ysfa near the head of the cwm.

Throughout the following day, Friday 18th, the weather was almost perfect. It was dry and sunny, but cold in the easterly winds. The party made a reasonably early start, leaving their tents soon after 9.30 a.m. with the intention of practising walking on snow and ice with crampons and ice-axes on the slopes at the foot of Amphitheatre Gully and, later in the morning, they climbed a frozen waterfall. They carried their lunch with them, planning to climb the gully soon after midday, which should have allowed enough time to complete their route and return to camp before dark.

Amphitheatre Gully may be seen as two distinct slopes, the lower part of about 100 metres being relatively easy-angled; the upper part, which included the *Left-hand Exit* route which they chose to climb, is almost 200 metres and is very steep with several near-vertical pitches. It is also very narrow. This upper part is graded II-III (Newcombe 1974), grade III being described as 'generally steep snow and ice in a succession of pitches – climbing of a serious standard.'

The leader of the party was Richard Palmer, aged 27, assisted by the other master, Robin Jenks, both of whom it seems had several years of experience, mainly walking and scrambling in the summer. Neither had previously visited Cwm Eigiau and they relied to a considerable extent on guide books. Most of the boys had gained some experience, again mostly on school walking and scrambling expeditions, and one or two had done some practice in ice-axe braking and the use of crampons in the Pyrenees the previous year. The total experience of the party was therefore somewhat limited and this trip was clearly designed to get as much experience in snow and ice work on steep slopes as the limited time available would allow.

Cwm Eigiau, Craig yr Ysfa, and Carnedd Llewellyn. The photograph was taken 24 hours after the accident and shows little snow and ice at this level.   *Royal Air Force*

The party was very well equipped. Much of their gear was in excellent condition and some items were brand new. Every member of the party had an ice-axe and was wearing crampons, but only four of them were wearing helmets.

After eating their lunch at the bottom of the gully, they started the climb in three groups of three, and from information given by the survivors it appears that they were for the most part moving in Alpine style, with about 10 metres of rope between each of the climbers in a group. There was about 5 metres of rope between the leader of a group and the last man in the group immediately above. About three-quarters of the way up, the leading group, consisting of Palmer, Jenks and a boy called Sam Dawes, arrived at a difficult area and Palmer told Jenks to lead on whilst he helped the other two groups across it. At about 4.25 p.m. Robin Jenks was near the top of the route with Richard Palmer, Dawes and the second and third groups directly in line below him in the gully. There was a crust over dry powdery snow of variable depth giving reasonably firm footholds, and where there was water ice, it

×: *Left hand exit.* O: *Jenks and the three injured boys were found here.* +: *Palmer and another injured boy came to rest here.*   *Tony Jones*

appeared hard. Jenks had noticed that at the top the snow was softer with less crust, but he was not experiencing any real difficulty. He suddenly found himself confronted by two boulders 3 to 4 feet high which had to be climbed over, and climbing 'delicately', he pushed his ice-axe into the snow above them, but there was no real belay. As he put his weight on the axe, the snow gave way and he began to slip. He managed to keep a firm grip on his axe and tried to stick it into some ice but that gave way too and he immediately came off and fell backwards. As he began to fall there were shouts of 'below', and then other shouts, but neither Palmer nor Dawes were able to hold him and were themselves pulled off. The whole group, in an avalanche of powdery snow, cannoned into the second group close behind, who were unable to take avoiding action in the narrow confines of the gully. They too were pulled off the slope, crashed into group number three and the whole party careered another 125 metres to the bottom of the slope. Robin Jenks and three boys, all of them injured, came to rest close together low down in the gully, level with the base of Amphitheatre Buttress, whilst Richard Palmer and another boy slid a further 15 metres down the scree.

Three boys who had escaped serious injury did all they could for their companions, and on the instructions of Robin Jenks, himself in great pain, they set off to get help. It was almost three hours before they reached the nearest telephone and the police were informed. Tony Jones, chairman and leader of the OVMRO, was notified of the accident at 7.20 p.m. and he immediately put the rescue operation into top gear. His first priority was to get essential information and two senior team members, Phil Williams-Jones and John Hulse, were soon interviewing the boys. Armed with the exact location, action could now be taken and C Flight, 22 Squadron RAF was airborne *en route* to the rescue base at Bryn Poeth in the Ogwen Valley within a very few minutes. The first party of team members started off for Cwm Eigiau on foot, whilst Tony Jones, accompanied by K. C. Gordon, were airlifted in. It was now about 8.20 p.m. After a short search they identified the accident site and, together with the winchman, Flight-Sergeant Jock Menmuir, they were lowered to the ground, close to where the two lower casualties were lying. They were quickly examined and essential first-aid given; then four of the injured were airlifted to hospital in Bangor. In the meantime every effort was made to resuscitate Richard Palmer and one of the boys, David Solomons, both of whom had suffered very severe head injuries, and as soon as the helicopter returned from its first trip to Bangor, these two were also evacuated to hospital. Sadly, they were both pronounced dead on arrival.

John Lindsay, OVMRO, on Oggie Base duty. *Tony Jones*

There remained the task of collecting all the equipment from the accident site and clearing up the base camp and getting it all back to the vehicle at Gwern Gof Isaf. This was done by members of the 'Oggie' team, assisted by the helicopter crew.

The actual cause of this tragic accident can best be attributed, in the words of an expert witness at the inquest, to 'sheer bad luck'. They were so near the end of the climb when the ice came away from the rock face, and a few more steps would have allowed them to belay properly and bring the whole party out safely. Subsidiary causes, all leading to the same effect, are for the reader to assess for himself. Perhaps the photographs provide a clue; were the ground conditions right for this type of training and was the expedition too ambitious for the level of experience of the party as a whole; perhaps they should have allowed more rope between the climbers in a group, and also kept each group further apart from each other; and perhaps in the narrow confines of the gully there were too many people too close together. Who knows the real answer? Probably it was the combined effect of all these things, but basically with a bit of luck it would never have happened.

It is a matter for conjecture and opinion as it must be with most mountain accidents, for hindsight gives one a wonderfully clear picture of cause and effect. However, if there is one lesson which seems to stand out very clearly, it is that a helmet may well have reduced the severity of the head injuries of Richard Palmer and David Solomons. David did not have one at all, and Richard lost his helmet as he fell.

It should be mentioned how valuable a part the helicopter and its crew played in this operation. Without the magnificent flying of the aircrew this rescue, in such an isolated place, would have taken very much longer and resulted in additional suffering to the injured. It is sad to record that the winchman, Jock Menmuir, lost his life a few years later whilst involved in a particularly difficult and dangerous rescue operation in the North Sea. One can only feel proud to have worked with men such as these.

"Moral Fibre and Self Rescue"

In military jargon 'lack of moral fibre' means no guts, or cowardice, and the same expression could well be used of some mountaineers who ape the more exhibitionist professional footballers – those who writhe in simulated agony at the tap of an ankle. The sort of mountaineer I refer to is the one who has a bit of a fall, or is feeling exhausted, and refuses to make any effort to get himself down to lower levels. He is quite happy to stay where he is until a rescue helicopter or MRT arrives to carry him down.

Of course, in most cases there will be a degree of shock and the casualty's ability to get himself down will be limited by his mental condition. There have been many instances where hill-walkers, who could at least have made an effort to get off the mountain, have panicked and been quite content to sit it out until rescued. I suspect that sometimes they realise, after they have rested for a while, that there is nothing really wrong with them and that all they needed was a rest and possibly a bit to eat.

One Saturday afternoon in February, after I had been to the summit of Snowdon in the morning in very cold and blustery conditions, I settled down in front of my log fire to watch the Wales vs England rugby match in Cardiff. It was a thrilling game, but at half-time the telephone rang and I was called out to an incident on the Glyders. The information was that a middle-aged woman had collapsed at Castell-y-Gwynt at about 1.00 p.m., and was thought to be suffering from hypothermia. In view of the weather, this was highly likely and the helicopter made several unsuccessful attempts to get up to her but was beaten back by the turbulence. Eventually a team from both the Llanberis and 'Oggie' MRTs went up to get her and found her in a fairly reasonable state. Because of the bad weather, her party had pressed on, looking for somewhere sheltered to eat their lunch, and it was well after 2.00 p.m. when the woman decided she had had enough and said she could go no further. By this time she was very cold and exhuasted, presumably because her party leader had not insisted on everyone eating something at the proper time.

It was almost 10.00 p.m. when the woman was carried into the bar at the Pen-y-Gwryd Hotel. "Ah, still open," she chirped as she jumped up off the stretcher. "Who wants a drink?" Out on the hill, one member of the MRT had fallen high up, and was in very considerable pain. He had torn a cartilage in his knee, but was determined not to disrupt the main rescue operation (at that time he was aware only that it was a case of hypothermia and for all he knew the casualty might be close to death). With another team member, he eventually crawled off the mountain and reached Pen-y-Gwryd at 2.00 a.m. A warden had waited to make sure the two men got safely down, having been in radio communication with them throughout their descent. Apart from the unselfish decision not to put the woman's life at any more risk, there was another reason why this man refused to ask for help. It was pride – the last thing he would have wanted was to be rescued by his own team! It would have taken a long time to live it down. There are many climbers and walkers who are aware of the risks they take, and do not wish to inflict the same risks on other people without good reason. These are the ones who can always be expected to make an attempt at self-rescue if they run into trouble.

Some years ago a walker tripped and fell descending the east ridge of Crib Goch. Luckily he managed to arrest his slide just before the top of the rock band. He lay there in great pain with a badly damaged knee which quickly swelled up like a football. To onlookers it seemed there was no question of him getting himself down, but he was adamant that he was going to try. Two people went down to Pen-y-Pass to get help, but the weather was too bad for a helicopter, and it was nearly two hours before the Llanberis MRT set off from the carpark at Pen-y-Pass. Twenty-five minutes later they reached Bwlch Moch where they found the injured man with his two companions. The casualty had made a tremendous effort to get himself off the mountain in spite of his very serious injury; it transpired that he had torn the ligaments in his knee and subsequently had to undergo surgical repair. To have dragged himself two hundred and fifty metres down a steep, rocky ridge, albeit helped by his companions, suffering the pain he did, showed great determination and guts. That is what is meant by moral fibre. The unfortunate man told us he had tried to get down to Pen-y-Pass on his own, "to save you blokes the bother of coming out to get me. But I couldn't manage another step and had to give it best."

Whether an injured or lost person gives way to panic depends on a number of factors, but principally on the state of his morale and will to survive. Age does not seem to make any difference, and fit young people are just as likely to attempt self-rescue as those of more mature years. The physical state of a person after an accident, the degree of shock, body temperature and of course the weather conditions can all play a significant

John Carter fell just out of sight behind the shoulder in the near foreground and eventually crawled across the rough and steep ground in the centre to the intersection and then down to Glaslyn. From there he followed the Miners Track and was found just short of the crushing mill on the side of Llyn Llydaw. Author

part in whether someone, whose normal moral fibre is beyond doubt, is able to try to help himself.

During the early Spring of 1987 SARDA was called out to look for 26-year-old John Carter who had left Pen-y-Pass Youth Hostel on his own in the morning and was seen heading up the Pyg Track towards Snowdon. He had not left any indication of his intended route, nor of his time of return to the hostel, so when he did not turn up for his evening meal the hostel staff were concerned. They asked the other hostellers if any of them had seen the young man, and a French student volunteered that he thought he had seen him at about 1.00 p.m. walking away from the path towards the snow-covered Clogwyn-y-Garnedd on the eastern side of Snowdon. This was the only clue and although we had no idea whether he had an ice-axe or crampons with him, the obvious conclusion was that he had intended to climb one of the gullies and unless he was a complete fool, he would have taken snow and ice equipment. At this stage, with nothing else to go on, we selected Clogwyn-y-Garnedd as the area of highest probability and set about searching it thoroughly before extending the operation to other areas.

The plan was for Heather Maling and her dog Spruce to go ahead up the Miners Track in Peter Walker's Land-rover to save walking-in time, whilst two more dog teams were to start up the Pyg Track and join Heather and Peter on Clogwyn-y-Garnedd. Soon after passing the crushing mill, Heather saw a 'bundle' lying at the side of the path. It was the missing man and, apart from being extremely cold and exhausted, he complained of pain in his leg, arm and across his back. After a quick check, Heather and Peter put him in the Land-rover and he was driven down to the hostel where a more thorough examination showed he had a boot-top fracture of his left leg and severe bruising of his right arm and back.

While we waited for an ambulance to arrive, he told us his story. He had started to climb solo up Central Trinity gully at about 2.00 p.m., and made good progress for half an hour before he put his axe into some soft snow which came away, hurling him 100 metres or so down the gully. Luckily he did not hit his head on any rocks during his fall and therefore remained conscious. As he lay at the bottom of the slope, he was aware of the pain getting worse as he got colder and colder. There were only three hours of daylight left and he comforted himself with the thought that 'the Rescue' would soon come out and get him. After some minutes a few flakes of snow began to fall and he began to shiver. Then he remembered that he had not told anyone where he had planned to climb and, as far as he knew, no-one had seen him leave the Pyg Track to come across to the gullies. Realising that the chances of the MRT coming to look for him were almost nil, at first he thought the best thing to do was to curl up and keep as warm as he could. But he had no food or drink and it became clear to him that in such conditions he would probably not survive the night. He therefore made up his mind to try to rescue himself; it was the only realistic option open to him. Unable to walk, he dragged himself across to the intersection of the Pyg Track and Miners Track, then down towards the crushing mill where he collapsed, unable to go any further. He had travelled not far short of two kilometres, including a descent of over 200 metres. It was a great effort by any standards and in spite of his basic mistakes, he deserved the highest praise.

The expression 'Self-Rescue' refers to people who have injured themselves and make the effort to get down without calling out official rescue teams. But in a broader context it would include a rescue carried out by other climbers or walkers, such as the incident on Snowdon in November 1987 which I have related in Chapter 16, Hypothermia. Many such rescues are successfully carried out every year and most of them are never reported.

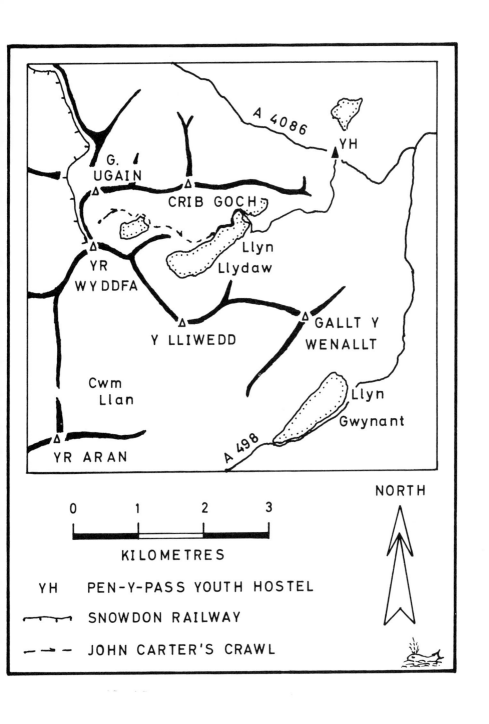

0	1	2	3

KILOMETRES

YH   PEN-Y-PASS YOUTH HOSTEL

⌐——┴——┐   SNOWDON RAILWAY

– ·– ·–   JOHN CARTER'S CRAWL

NORTH

Not long after I joined the Llanberis MRT and became a voluntary warden, I was involved in such a rescue on Snowdon with Meirion Thomas who, like me, had only recently joined the team. Meirion lived and worked on Anglesey, although he was, as he used proudly to say, "a local boy", having been brought up in Llanberis. Over the years Meirion has been one of that band of team members who are always there, whether it be for a training session, or the real thing. In every MRT there is a hard core of people like Meirion who can always be relied upon, but this cannot be said of a fair proportion of members who tend to please themselves and only turn out for training exercises which they think will be the most fun. For example, an exercise with helicopters which will involve winching into the aircraft, having a flight round the mountains and being winched down again, can be guaranteed to produce a full turn-out. A routine stretcher-lower, for example, would probably only be attended by the hard core of 'regulars' and it follows therefore that the success of a team depends very much on the Meirions of this world.

The incident happened at Easter 1979. The snow still lay deep above six hundred metres, and frequent snow showers continued to fall over the weekend. I had met up with Meirion on the summit of Snowdon. He had come up over Crib Goch and Crib-y-Ddysgl ridges and we decided to return to Pen-y-Pass together. As we started down The Zigzags it began to snow again, but the shower was short-lived although the cloud persisted and visibility was very poor in the mist. A party of SARDA handlers on an exercise passed us on their way up to the summit, but apart from them we saw no one about. Just short of the intersection we took off our crampons. But before we set off again, we heard a single, loud cry – **Help**. It was difficult to be certain from which direction the shout came, so we stopped and listened for a repeat. We did not wait long and both of us turned towards the gully between The Zigzags and Trinity. Again the cry came, confirming the general direction and I shouted back that help was on its way, but to go on calling so that we could identify his position.

Meirion and I retraced our steps and as we climbed back up towards The Zigzags, the voice came more and more from our left and so we traversed towards the gully. There were some fresh footprints in the snow which seemed to follow others which might have been made earlier in the day. We were still short of the gully itself and the voice was now definitely coming from directly above us, probably not far short of the ridge. We climbed out of the soft snow onto firmer going and came to a shoulder which was completely iced over. Yet the footmarks went straight over it and disappeared up the steep slope into the mist. Having re-fixed our crampons, we negotiated the shoulder and pressed on towards the voice, now 'strength five' and obviously not many metres away from us. Suddenly we saw our quarry, which turned out to be two people stuck on the iced-up crags just below the ridge. They were a young couple who happened to be on their honeymoon in Caernarfon and had decided to spend the day, which had started fine and bright, climbing Snowdon. They had absolutely no idea of the conditions and had not even a semblance of the right equipment nor indeed clothing for such an expedition. They had followed the other footmarks thinking they were still on the Pyg Track, and had scrambled somehow over the ice-shoulder and finally got stuck, unable to move either forwards or backwards in the rocks where we found them. They had quickly become very cold and too frightened to move. It did not seem that anyone else had heard their shouts and, thinking that the SARDA party might still be within earshot, we blew the distress signal on our whistles. But no-one responded and in fact the SARDA group had long since left the summit to go down the Watkin Path to Lliwedd.

It took a lot of patience and coaxing to get the young bride to move. She had completely frozen in both senses – scared out of her mind and physically cold and stiff. I always carried a walking rope in my rucksack, in case of just such a need, and I belayed to the crag whilst Meirion tied the girl on and led her down. Some way beyond the shoulder they stopped and untied the rope. I then repeated the operation with the man and, after leaving him with Meirion, I went back to release the belay. Coming back over the shoulder, I made a mistake even experienced mountaineers can sometimes make; I put one crampon too near the other and they locked together. It was a nasty moment, and it took me several minutes before I managed to free my feet. All the stamping and so on had formed a ball of snow between the spikes of each crampon and, as soon as I started walking again, my feet shot from under me and I was immediately in a free slide. My axe did not hold in the soft snow and so I threw myself on to my back hoping that my rucksack would build up a bank of snow in front of it and act as a brake. It worked and I came to a stop alongside Meirion and the couple, whom I can still picture standing open-mouthed with amazement.

After we had given them something to eat and drink, they soon recovered and we walked them safely down to Pen-y-Pass. It was almost dark as we bade them good-bye and, having thanked us enthusiastically, they went on their way to carry on with their honeymoon. For them that will be a day to remember, but I wonder if they realise how lucky they were that Meirion and

I just happened to be in the right place at the right time. It might have turned out so differently, even tragically.

Although this rescue involved two MRT members, it was not classed as an incident because the police had not been informed and therefore had not authorised the team to turn out. Over the years there have been many life-saving rescues which have gone unnoticed and unsung, and many of them have been carried out by National Park wardens in the course of their duty on the mountains. I believe that all incidents should be reported to the police so that they can be included in the official statistics. Only then can there be a true picture of the Mountain Rescue scene.

"Equipment"

Equipment of itself does not make people instant mountaineers, yet it is a matter of constant amazement how many inexperienced walkers and climbers go into the mountains armed with map and compass, or crampons and ice-axe, firmly believing that these things are passports to safety. They are no such thing; and it must be the keynote of safety in mountains to learn how to use your equipment correctly under safe conditions before setting out. The wonder is that so many people ignore this obvious advice and get away with it; sadly, though, many do not.

No one is safe in the mountains if he cannot use his map and compass properly and with confidence, and it follows therefore that everyone, whether in a group with a good and experienced leader, or walking with a friend, should have sufficient knowledge to find his way around should they become separated, or if, for some reason, the leader cannot continue.

From time to time we get almost arctic conditions in Snowdonia and aspiring alpinists come over in droves to try their hand at snow and ice climbing in conditions which they would otherwise have to go to the Alps to experience. Amongst them, of course, are many who have done it all before and are well enough versed in the required skills to tackle the conditions safely. For the rest, though, it probably means a quick visit to one of the climbing-gear shops where they spend a lot of money on an ice-axe and crampons, and maybe on other items which they do not need at this stage. But it all helps to build up the image! Then they are away up to the icy tops. Very few of them bother to ask someone experienced in this sort of climbing to spare a few minutes to show them the basics, such as how to fix on their crampons correctly, how to carry the ice-axe and how to arrest a fall with it. Even this limited instruction would be a help and would give them something to build on. The fault lies with the novice who thinks it's all so easy and not with the old hands, who in most cases would be only too pleased to pass on the benefit of their knowledge and experience so that others can enjoy the Alpine conditions more safely.

Many years ago I was leading a group of cadets up Ben Lui in Scotland. We were walking head-on into a strong, freezing wind and conditions were nothing less than arctic. When we reached the snow line we stopped to put on our crampons and, a minute or so after restarting, I heard an ominous 'clank' as one of the cadets' crampons fell off. I had joined the camp only the previous evening and had been assured that all the boys had been instructed in, and had practised, putting on their crampons, ice-axe techniques and so on. But this cadet must have been the inattentive one and he had simply no idea. "Shall I go on with one crampon?" he asked me. By the time I had put his crampon on properly and re-fixed the other one, I had no feeling left in my fingers and was scared that I might get a touch of frost-bite. Apart from that we were all getting very chilled and as the weather got worse and a blizzard blew up, I aborted the climb and we retraced our steps to the vehicle.

Another important point is that, whether or not you have learned the techniques properly, there is absolutely no point in having the necessary equipment with you unless it is ready for immediate use, and it is equally irresponsible to venture into difficult areas without the essential items of gear for the expedition in hand.

During Easter weekend in the early 1970s, an incident occurred on Snowdon which horrified the whole mountaineering fraternity. A party of fifteen schoolboys from a public school in the South of England, under the leadership of four masters, had climbed to the summit of Snowdon. There was still snow and ice covering the mountains, and conditions required the proper equipment and knowledge of how to use it correctly. On their way down the railway line heading for Llanberis, three of the boys slid over the edge at a notoriously dangerous spot called Clogwyn Goch, about which there is more in the next chapter. When the boys walked unawares on to the convex slope of packed frozen snow which filled the cutting, nothing could stop them sliding over the edge – **except an ice-axe**. But the whole party of nineteen had only two axes between them and one of the boys who was carrying one of them did, in fact, arrest his slide with it and thereby saved his life. At the inquest on the three boys, expert witnesses stated that in such conditions everyone going on to the mountains should carry an ice-axe and be proficient in its use. They stressed that, with only two axes, this party should not have been taken up there at all.

On February 14th 1983, a headline in the *Liverpool Daily Post* (Welsh News) proclaimed, 'Rescue Chief's Fury after Peak Tragedy.' There followed a report quoting John Ellis Roberts, the Head Warden and leader of the Llanberis MRT involved in the incident, as saying that a climber, George Kormoss, and his two companions, all of whom came from

Merseyside, had set out to tackle Crib Goch and Crib-y-Ddysgl ridges without the equipment necessary for the difficult conditions high up. The ridges were covered with hard-packed frozen snow and the wardens had put up weather forecasts and notices warning about the dangerous ground conditions at the start of all the main paths to the summit of Snowdon, but this trio had either not seen them, or chosen to ignore them. The three men, none of whom had ice-axes or crampons, had managed to get across Crib Goch with some difficulty and much trepidation, but they decided to press on beyond Bwlch Goch, leaving their last possible escape route behind them. Immediately above *Fantail Gully* on the north side of Crib-y-Ddysgl, Kormoss, who was about 25 metres ahead of his friends, slipped and slid down the packed ice in the gully on his stomach, and disappeared over the edge, crashing 150 metres into Cwm Glas. If he had had an ice-axe and known the correct technique, he could have arrested his fall. Without one, he did not stand a chance. He was killed on impact, with extensive head injuries.

The following year a similar accident, with almost identical cause and effect, occurred on Crib Goch, which was icy and treacherous for the inexperienced. A party of seven young teenagers with an adult leader, all from the London area, were crossing the ridge when thirteen year-old Jonathan Bevis slipped and fell 150 metres to his death. He was described by his father as "very adventurous – climbing was one of his favourite hobbies." He had his own ice-axe, but for some unknown reason it remained strapped to his rucksack instead of being in his hand ready for immediate use if required. One of his friends who had just bought himself a new axe and was keen to try it out, was practising carrying it as he walked across the ridge. Possibly momentarily unbalanced by seeing Jonathan slip over the edge, this boy also slipped, but immediately used his axe to arrest the slide and he remained on the ridge, still alive. Had Jonathan been carrying his axe in his hand he could have used it to try to save himself and the chances are that he would still be alive today.

John Ellis Roberts, who was leading this rescue operation, described the tragedy as "sad and ironic that the party was fairly well equipped, but not wearing crampons." But I must stress again that however good the equipment, it is useless unless one knows how to use it, and has it ready for use should it be needed.

These two stories relate to equipment required for winter conditions, but whether you are walking or climbing in winter or summer, certain guidelines can be laid down for those items of equipment considered to be essential. It is not my purpose to include a detailed list of them as this can be found in any good book on mountaincraft. However, a good strong pair of boots with an adequate tread must be the number one requirement for walkers. Shoes, trainers or bumper boots give little or no support to the ankle over rough ground, whilst flip-flops or sandals, which are frequently seen on Snowdon during the holiday season (and I have even seen them when there was snow on the ground!) are worse than useless; they are dangerous and are 'an accident waiting to happen'.

In chapter 20, 'The Right To Risk One's Life', is the story of a party of climbers on Idwal Slabs in November 1982 when nineteen-year-old Archie Cameron fell and was killed. At the inquest the Coroner severely criticised the party on four counts. A report of the inquest appeared in a national newspaper under the heading 'Coroner lists climbers' four grave errors' and gave them as follows:–

They had failed to notify anyone of their intention to climb on the Slabs, so no one knew they were there;

They had not checked the weather forecast;

Their knowledge and experience of climbing was poor and not up to the standard of the climb they were attempting;

They had only the very minimum of clothing, no waterproofs (although the weather forecast had correctly warned of rain overnight), and Cameron himself was not wearing any form of mountaineering or climbing boots as he preferred to wear pumps.

A torch should always be high on the list of priorities in case you run out of daylight and have to find your way down in the dark. Of course, this is far more important during the winter, but it is also a good idea in the autumn and summer, as the next two anecdotes illustrate.

The first incident happened on October 25th 1981, when a search was mounted for three people, all aged between thirty-five and forty, who had failed to turn up after setting out to walk across the snow-covered Glyders from Ogwen Cottage up the Devil's Kitchen and over to Pen-y-Gwryd. After waiting until 8.00 p.m. for them to reach the hotel, a party from the Llanberis MRT, including myself and my search dog Gwynne, set off up the Miners Track to follow their route in reverse direction. After two hours of slow progress, Gwynne alerted to a scent high up on the south side of the Glyders and we found them stumbling towards us in the dark. They were quite safe and well, but tired and frustrated after struggling through showers of sleet and snow over the boulder-strewn summits. They were well-equipped for such an expedition, and all of them had torches. But not one of them had checked their batteries before setting out, nor had they spares with them. Long before we found them groping their way down in the pitch-black night, the last torch had flickered and died. So to 'torches' as an essential item of equipment, add 'and spare batteries'.

The second incident occurred on August 11th 1982 when a forty-eight-year-old teacher and his son, aged twenty-two, from Manchester were climbing on Gyrn Las on the south side of the Llanberis Pass near Cwm Glas. They were still a long way from the top when darkness fell and, because there was no moon and it was a particularly black night, they were unable to move either up or down. The two men were reported missing soon after dark, and the MRT turned out to look for them. Phil Benbow's dog, Jet, alerted at the foot of Gyrn Las and indicated their position high up the face, and a helicopter, using its searchlight, came in and winched both men to safety. They were experienced climbers and were properly equipped, so what went wrong? Quite simple – they had not allowed enough time to complete the route in daylight and neither of them had a torch.

"Clogwyn Goch – The Killer Convex"

The tragic incident I recalled in the previous chapter, when three schoolboys slipped to their death from the railway cutting at Clogwyn Goch, was only one in a whole catalogue of fatal accidents at this spot, going back as far as local mountaineers can remember. There was a good reason why this short length of the line – no more than twenty metres, in fact – was called the 'killer convex' and, in my very early days on expeditions to Snowdonia, I remember my leaders warning us to avoid the railway line when there was packed snow. The cutting across the west face of Carnedd Ugain is at its narrowest at this point and the snow builds up against the back wall, forming a convex slope down to the outside edge of the cutting and to a two-hundred-metre drop into Cwm d'ur Arddu. Any one walking along the railway line on either side of Clogwyn Goch is on ground which is relatively safe, as the cutting is much wider and it is easier to keep well away from the edge; but unless they are aware of the way the snow and ice builds up along the narrow stretch, they walk straight on to it and are likely to slip over the edge. Whether or not such a slip is fatal depends largely on the amount of snow lying on the ground and there have been many miraculous escapes because the victim has bounced from one pocket of snow to another, finally landing on a sufficient depth of snow at the bottom to absorb the momentum of his fall. But when the snow pockets are not there, usually towards the end of the winter around Easter, and when there is still snow and ice on the line, the fall is almost certainly fatal.

In the story of 'The Heroes of the Glass Mountain' in February 1979, thirty-six-year-old James Watkinson had one of those lucky escapes. He had been cushioned by the blanket of snow as he fell, and despite head injuries he had managed to crawl several hundred metres to the shelter of a stone wall where he spent a cold and restless night. As he made his way to the wall, he left a trail of blood in the snow which was spotted from a helicopter early the following morning. The crew saw Watkinson waving weakly to them, and soon had him on board and heading for Bangor hospital where he quickly recovered.

Two years later, just after Christmas in 1981, the convex was completely

The cutting at Clogwyn Goch showing how the convex slope is formed as the snow builds up across the railway lines. The 200 metre drop into Cwm d'ur Arddu starts at the coping stones in the centre of the picture.   *Author*

iced over and was like a miniature curving glacier. A party of Venture Scouts was walking down the railway line towards Llanberis when seventeen-year-old Simon Wombwell from Cambridgeshire stepped on to the icy slope, slipped and in a split second went over the edge and fell into the cwm below. The party was properly equipped, but Simon lost his ice-axe as he tried to arrest his slide with it. He scarcely had time to get the axe into the correct position, but in any case it was wrenched out of his hands as he tried to dig the pick into the hard ice. Thoroughly shaken, two of Simon's companions made their way down into the cwm, and told the rest of the group to get on down to Llanberis as fast as they could to raise the alarm. At this stage they did not know whether Simon was still alive, or how badly injured he might be. The Llanberis MRT was called out and it was well after dark when I was sent ahead of the main party with my search dog Gwynne and a First-aider, Colin Dickinson, to try to locate the casualty.

Soon after we had left the Llanberis path at the bottom of Allt Moses, Gwynne alerted and sped off ahead to make her 'find'. We followed her in and soon saw a dim torch ahead of us with Simon and his two companions close to the base of the cliffs. We were relieved to find him conscious and in remarkably good shape considering his fall and the length of time he had been lying out there in such extreme cold. A quick examination suggested that he had broken his left leg, and had chest injuries. I radioed back to the team leader asking for a helicopter to be scrambled if possible, as Simon was in a lot of pain and speed was vital. The main body of the MRT soon arrived and we strapped Simon to the stretcher ready for winching if the helicopter managed to come in close enough.

In spite of repeated efforts, the pilot could not make it as he had no horizon due to the white background. His difficulty was compounded by an over-zealous team member who let off a flare as the helicopter came in close, which completely blinded the pilot and brought forth a stream of invective! And that was the end of the helicopter's part in the operation for the rest of the night. The team now had to carry the stretcher across the frozen snow slopes to the road-head at Hafodty, an operation which took almost three hours, and Simon was transferred to an ambulance and quickly driven to Bangor hospital. Next morning he had recovered enough to meet the Press and describe his fall through space. "It was very steep, with rocks and boulders jutting out of the snow," he said. "I struggled to avoid them and it was a nightmare until I lost consciousness . . . " As his brother Richard said, "It's incredible he's still alive".

During April 1986 conditions on Snowdon were particularly severe and in the space of a few days no fewer than three walkers fell from Clogwyn Goch, and all survived because of the thick blanket of snow. Apart from their survival – one of them escaped with nothing worse than a cut chin – they had one other thing in common, that not one of them had an ice-axe or crampons. Without them they should never have been up there in those conditions in the first place.

Within that same short period another walker, also without an ice-axe and crampons, was walking along the line of the Llanberis path across the exposed and ice-covered slope above the railway cutting. Most of the snow had been blown off here, leaving an extremely slippery and dangerous ice-cap. The thirty-seven-year-old man was with friends from the Southport Fell-Walking Club, and was said later to have been a very careful and experienced fell walker; but we are bound to wonder how much 'mountain walking' he had done, in severe winter conditions? Were he as experienced as was claimed, it is beyond comprehension why he was walking across this ice-cap wearing only rubber-soled boots. Inevitably he slipped and shot away down the hill. By the time he reached the railway line, he was travelling so fast that he shot out into space and missed the cushioning effect of the snow

A warning notice at the lower end of the Clogwyn Goch section of the railway. The Llanberis Path is clearly visible as it contours under Carnedd Ugain.   *Author*

pockets which had effectively saved the lives of the previous three walkers. Sadly he was killed outright, and it remained only for members of the MRT to go out to recover his body.

It cannot be stressed too strongly that there is no comparison between summer and winter hill-walking – a fact which is underlined by the wording of the Mountain Leadership Certificate (Summer) which states, 'Training was not given in leadership in snow and ice conditions.' For anyone who wants to lead groups in British mountains in winter, a special leadership course and certificate is available.

Within the last ten years the Mountain Railway management, in concert with the National Park, has tried to keep walkers away from Clogwyn Goch by erecting notices at a height of about a metre above the actual line, and at points well to the north and south of the dangerous stretch. The first notices had little or no effect, and I have frequently seen walkers in winter reading the words directing them to the Llanberis path, and then deliberately ignoring them and walking on towards the 'killer convex'. When I have asked them "Why?" the usual reply was either that they thought it was warning them about trains – a likely story with possibly a metre of snow on the the line – or more truthfully that they would risk it. The notices have recently been greatly improved, and they now leave no doubt about what they mean, but you will always get the 'smart Alecs' who ignore anything designed to make their going a bit safer, and who seem to regard the notices as an unwelcome intrusion into their freedom to go and do as they please.

The Head

All Search and Rescue activities are usually treated very seriously, but every now and then some little incident happens which causes amusement and temporarily lifts the aura of gloom and doom which normally surrounds these operations. They usually occur on searches for missing people, when unsuspecting couples are not infrequently found in comprising situations. They do not bargain for the 'all-seeing' nose of the search dog finding them in a small tent hidden away in a well-reconnoitred position, convinced they are safe from prying eyes! It is tough luck, and of course they seldom see the funny side.

During a particularly hot period during the summer of 1980, SARDA was asked to look for a missing head on the east side of the Snowdon Gribin. This was a most unusual and gruesome job, but it was done on the instructions of the Coroner to whom the death of a headless female body had been reported two days earlier. One of the Park wardens had been working his way down the Gribin when he paused to look down the pricipitous east side into Llyn Llydaw. He spotted something coloured lying a hundred and twenty metres down on what looked like a narrow ledge. There was no way down from where he was and he had to go down to the lakeside and climb up to see what it was. When he reached the ledge, he could see that it was the body of a walker and the colour was an anorak. It was obvious it had been lying there for some time as it was partially decomposed and was very unpleasant indeed. The body was wedged between rocks and when he tried to lift it to look at the head, there was none! Whoever it was must have fallen head first from the ridge above and hit the cliff a bit higher up, where the head had been wrenched off. The torso had continued down and had come to rest on the ledge where the warden found it. After a quick look around, he saw no sign of the head and came down to report what he had found. The police and Coroner were informed and the headless body was recovered.

The Coroner explained that he could not hold an inquest unless the head was produced as there would be nothing to show whether death had been caused by an accidental fall or by bodily harm inflicted by some person unknown. Roland Layland, Heather Maling and I were asked to search an area on the side of the Gribin, but for some reason we were not properly briefed and it was too far to the north of the position where the body, now known to be that of a woman, had been found. In effect, therefore, we were wasting our time as far as finding the missing head was concerned, but it was a gorgeous day and it was all very useful practice as we covered the whole area from the shore of the lake to the ridge.

The night before the search, Roland had surprised a small teenage boy who had broken into his home, and chased him to a nearby centre for delinquent youngsters. As a punishment the principal ordered the lad, whom we will call John, to accompany Roland on the search next day. John duly turned up, an undersized, ginger-haired, fourteen-year-old Cockney. He was far from mountain-fit, but managed to keep up with the search and barely spoke a word until lunch-time. We were sitting on the ridge in bright sunshine, thoroughly enjoying the views towards Shropshire, the utter peace

Roland Layland   *Keith Brown*

and the warmth of the sun, but I suppose we were all thinking more about the dead woman and what had actually happened and, as so often happens, the day was darkened by the reason for our being there.

After resting for a few moments and taking the edge off his appetite, the little Cockney suddenly found his tongue and became interested in what he was doing, in the dogs, the mountains and the view. For a while we thought he would never stop talking, but then he paused and seemed to be deep in thought. "It ain't right, yer know," he began again, "it ain't right." "What isn't right, John?" I asked him. "What we're doin 'ere," he said. "That 'ead's looking at us all the time. Why can't we go away and leave 'er in peace? If we disturb 'er she'll come and 'aunt us. I'm scared; I know the 'ead's somewhere watching us." Young John was deadly serious, and I can still see the look of fear in his eyes as he thought of the ever watchful 'ead 'aunting him. When we had finished our task and started the walk back to Pen-y-Pass, John was visibly relieved. "I'm glad we didn't find 'er," he said. "She'd never 'ave forgiven us and then she'd 'ave 'aunted us." We talked of many other things on the way down, but the insight I had had into a little Cockney boy's mind was as revealing as, in a way, it was amusing. At any rate, whilst I listened to him chattering on about being watched and 'aunted, the dark side of the day lifted for a while and made it, on the whole, quite an enjoyable experience.

Next day the wardens climbed the cliff above the ledge where the body had come to rest and, quite a way up, they found the missing head – by now only a skull. It was wedged firmly in a fissure in the rocks and it must have been at this point that the body had been torn away and continued down to the ledge. It was all very gruesome, but there was no evidence of foul play. The woman was traced and found to have been reported missing eight weeks earlier. She had been walking alone and had bought some souvenirs in the summit café. There was no indication that her fall and death was anything other than an accident, and the Coroner brought in a verdict of 'death by misadventure'.

SOS Unanswered

It was another scorching-hot day in June 1981 and, after a busy Sunday-lunch session in the hotel, I took Gwynne up the Miners Track as far as Glaslyn and back. Two hours' walking in that heat was quite enough!

As I came back into the carpark at Pen-y-Pass at about 4.30 p.m., Harvey Lloyd, warden of the youth hostel there and also my group co-ordinator in the Llanberis MRT, came across the road to meet me. "I'm glad I've caught you, Bob," he said. "We've got a report of a body lying under the crags below Cwm Glas. I've collected a few blokes together with a stretcher, and the police are waiting at Blaenant. Can you possibly take charge and do the necessary?" "Sure I can, Harvey," I replied, and made my way down the Pass to Blaenant. I had heard that just after dark on the previous Thursday, three separate reports of a light flashing persistently, high up in the Cwm Glas area, had been phoned in to the police. An MRT member and a police car had each driven up and down the Pass several times, but had not seen any sign of a light and, shortly before 2.00 a.m., they decided it was probably a youngster fooling about. At the same time, asleep in their beds in Llanberis, there were four SARDA handlers, all able to go out to investigate the reported light; but they were not called and remained unaware of the drama which unfolded and spent itself high up in the cwm. I was one of those sleeping handlers.

At this time we were still fighting for recognition as a credible organisation and the team member who drove up and down the Pass that night had no idea that the dog handlers, all of whom were members of the same MRT anyway, were asleep only ten minutes' drive away, and would have given almost anything to be called out and have the chance of locating the flashing light. And the police did not know either.

I met our local policeman who was not far off retirement age and was amazed that, in spite of the heat, he was in his full uniform. I had a camera with me to take the necessary photographs which would be required by police HQ, but our policeman insisted on climbing up to where the body had been reported. He was clearly suffering and I was worried that he was going to have a heart attack. Eventually I told him, unequivocally, not to come any

The dead man had fallen from the top of the crag. His body and battered torch were found on the scree where an MRT member is seen searching for other items.   *Author*

further and that I would take the photographs. He did not take much persuading and was glad to be able to sit down and wait for us to bring the body down on the stretcher. The casualty was a young man in his early twenties. He was clearly not a mountaineer and was wearing a light-weight bush-shirt and drill slacks, and a pair of not very strong walking shoes, but with an adequate tread. He lay face downwards, and the heat during the three days he had lain there, and the ravages of blow-flies, made the job of recovering his body most unpleasant and nauseating. I took a series of photographs and then looked round for any pieces of equipment or clues of any sort. His broken torch lay only a few feet up the scree. We wrapped his open injuries and then stretchered him down to a waiting hearse on the road, collecting our policeman on the way.

Next day I was asked to walk up into Cwm Glas with another police officer to see if we could identify where the dead man had been flashing his torch.

Back in the cwm, we found a small unoccupied tent in which were the remains of an evening meal – plate, knife, fork and mug – all of which had been used and pushed to one side to be washed up later. The sleeping bag was zipped up and had not been slept in recently and, between the tent, which was in a sheltered hollow, and the top of the cliff directly above the place where the young man had come to rest, we picked up a cheap type of compass. The police officer and I agreed that the victim had probably eaten his supper and then, in the fading light, had wandered down past Llyn Glas towards the cliff top from where he would be able to watch the sun set across Anglesey. We could only assume that, having ventured a bit too far down, he had found that he could not get back up the crag and had then started to flash his SOS signal – an appeal to the world down below to come and help him. But nobody came, and the most likely scenario was that either he lost his grip, or tried to scramble back up, slipped, and fell. As we pictured the young man's agony of mind and probable panic, we could both imagine all too vividly his despair when no one answered his cry for help.

If we were right in pinpointing his position near the cliff top, he would have fallen into 'dead ground' where his light could not possibly have been seen from the road. As it was, it may well be that he was still shrieking for help after the watchers on the road had decided there was no one there. We will never know for certain, but today no one would hesitate to call the dogs out to investigate lights flashing at night or cries for help heard coming out of cloud or fog. SARDA insists that every handler would far rather be called out to go and have a look than be left undisturbed only to find, as I did, a few days later, that someone had died because his SOS went unanswered.

Why Search is an Emergency

The aim of every rescue operation is to save someone's life and, whether it occurs at sea or on land, underground or high up in the mountains, the first priority is to stabilise the condition of injured or sick people and do everything possible to ensure their ultimate recovery. In out-of-the-way places such as mountains and moorlands the speed with which these people can be brought to safety is the crux of the problem, and time is the all-important factor. But since a rescue cannot begin until the whereabouts of the casualty are known, finding him as quickly as possible takes precedence over everything else and Search becomes an Emergency. This is especially so in bad weather when the condition of a casualty is likely to be in danger of rapid deterioration.

A relatively simple injury such as a broken leg presents no problems when it happens within the environs of a town or village, possibly on the football pitch, where the casualty can be stretchered to the touchline and be in an ambulance on the way to hospital within a few minutes. When it happens on an exposed mountainside, where side-effects such as shock or hypothermia are factors to be reckoned with, the same injury becomes a serious and urgent problem. Here there is no stretcher on the touchline, nor an ambulance within a few minutes' call. It can be two or three hours before the informant reaches a telephone and at least as long again before the advance party of the rescue team starts first-aid treatment. Meantime it must be assumed that the casualty needs emergency care, and the speed with which he is found will be instrumental in his chances of survival.

In the mountains no action can be taken to find and recover an injured or sick person until either a companion comes down to report the incident, which can take two hours or more, or the person is reported overdue by someone who knows the time he should have returned to his base. In the first case the informant will usually be able to tell the team leader the location of the casualty, and a rescue operation will be mounted without delay. Sometimes, however, the informant leaves the scene without establishing the exact position of the injured or sick person, and this usually happens when he has suffered shock after witnessing a nasty accident. The normal reaction is one of panic, and to dash off to get help, whereas it would be much more helpful for the rescue services to get a clear 'fix' of the location before leaving the scene. If the informant has no map with which to establish a reasonably accurate reference, then he should take careful note of prominent features, and relate the position of the casualty to them. I have known informants who have had no clear idea of where they have been walking in the first place, and it is surprising how often members of walking groups are content to follow their leader without even knowing which mountain they are on!

If the informant cannot give an exact location, one of two things may happen. In fine weather, he will be able to point the MRT in the right direction, and in good visibility they should be able to gain visual contact very quickly. A group of people standing around on a mountainside is very obvious to an observer whether he is on the ground or in the air. On the other hand, the accident may have happened in poor visibility, or the weather may have deteriorated after the informant left the casualty, and you are then faced with a serious search situation, especially if the informant has told you that the casualty is badly injured and needs urgent attention. In this situation, or when someone is reported missing, or cries for help have been heard in the clouds, and no-one has seen the incident, a crisis point has been reached and a search must be carried out before the first-aiders and

John Grisdale (right) and John Jackson disembarking from the helicopter at Pen-y-Pass.
John B. Jackson colln.

Chris Whermby and his dog at Pen-y-Pass after completing a high-level search.
John B. Jackson colln.

stretcher-party can be committed to the hill. To deploy them to help in the actual search, possibly on a hunch that the person might be in a certain area, could mean that they are nowhere near when they are most badly needed.

A rescue operation can be either straightforward when the team goes into action immediately, or it must be preceded by a search to establish the precise position of the casualty, and this can sometimes take hours, even days. In good visibility, and subject to availability, an immediate rescue is nowadays frequently done by the RAF Search and Rescue helicopter flight of 22 Squadron stationed permanently at Valley, only ten minutes' flying time away on Anglesey. Search is an emergency and an urgent response to the informant's plea for help is the first requirement.

Most searches take place after dark when people are reported overdue, and usually in bad weather. In these cases it is normal practice to wait an hour or two, depending on the circumstances and conditions, because a large proportion of overdue people, who may well have been lost, manage to find their way off the mountain even if they are miles away from where they intended to come down. A phone call is all that is required for a search call-out to be cancelled and a lot of wasted effort and expense saved. Sadly many people do not think of letting someone back at their base know what has

*A representative picture of the various organisations which make up a major search. Front
(l to r): Local police, helicopter crew and paramedic, Police mobile canteen vehicle and staff.
Centre: civilian and Service MRTs, National Park wardens, and their vehicles. Rear: Police
radio communications vehicle and a Whirlwind helicopter (now long since replaced by the
Wessex). This photograph was taken many years ago, before SARDA had become established.
Today there would probably be at least ten search dog teams in addition to the units
represented here.*   *North Wales Police*

happened, and the first time it is known that they are safe and well is when
they have journeyed back to where they meant to be in the first place.

As soon as the 'waiting period' is finished, the search must be started with
all speed. By this time it is highly probable that the missing person really is in
trouble and may be in desperate need of help. If he is not injured and is
wandering about trying to find his way to safety, a predictable pattern of
action begins to develop. It is an even chance that, as he roams, he will be
getting farther and farther away from his base, and as he does so the search
area automatically increases in size. To start with, the search area is basically
a circle with a radius equal to the maximum possible distance the missing
person could have moved from his base during his walk. The longer he is out
there, the farther away he could be and the search area theoretically gets
larger from hour to hour. The chances of success are therefore far greater
early on when the search area is at its smallest.

Sam Roberts and Brian Jones make final adjustments to the stretcher before winching. The winchman, yellow helmet, waits alongside.   *John B. Jackson colln.*

The urgency of the search demands that, if possible, it should begin straight away and continue throughout the night and, now that SARDA is available, the practice of waiting until first light to begin the operation is no longer acceptable. Human searchers are of limited use at night or in bad visibility. They have to seek with their eyes, and this limitation depends on the length of their torch beams and the actual visibility at the time. In general terms a human searcher would have to walk extremely close to a casualty or a lost person asleep in a hollow, perhaps almost hidden by heather or bracken, to be sure of finding them. I remember one search in particular when the footsteps of a searcher passed within a couple of feet of where a lost orienteer was lying asleep with a sprinkling of snow over him, which was very effective camouflage. The searcher completely failed to see him. The acceptance of SARDA has changed all that and, in normal conditions, one well-trained dog is equal to at least twenty human searchers. The stories of searches in this book show how the use of dogs has developed over the years. Search techniques merit serious study and the training programme carried through by SARDA (Wales) includes all the factors which might affect a dog's scenting ability, such as wind, air, and ground temperature, terrain, humidity, rain, snow, fog and so on. The programme also covers how to plan the complete coverage of a given search area and, more recently, the

Horizontal Thomas stretcher being winched. Note the position of the winchman where he can re-assure the casualty and help to control the stretcher when they reach the open door of the helicopter.   *Harvey Lloyd*

actual organisation of a search operation.

The use of RAF helicopters in search and rescue operations has become an invaluable aid to quicker and more effective searches. Not only do they carry out intensive overflying of designated areas, but they frequently airlift searchers, including the dog teams, which undergo special winching training, to start their operation high up in the mountains. This increases the effectiveness of ground parties and makes the best use of their time and energy by getting them as far up the hill as possible into their allotted search areas. In Snowdonia this means a saving of up to two hours or more otherwise spent walking-in. The same applies to members of teams actually involved in a rescue, but in many instances the helicopter crew will go straight in, lower the winchman, who will carry out first-aid and, having winched the stretchered casualty and winchman into the aircraft, fly to hospital, all within a relatively short time. Such help is invaluable not only to members of MRTs who in most cases have to leave their work to answer the call, but more importantly to the casualty who will have a far greater chance of survival than would otherwise have been the case. Once the search or rescue is over, the helicopter usually returns to the scene of the incident and, whenever possible, recovers the dog teams and rescue personnel who are then available to answer another call for help. The contribution that RAF helicopters have made to search and rescue operations in the mountains has been profound and in the past few years the whole concept of such operations has changed.

Another factor which has transformed the efficiency of rescue teams has been the improvement in communications. Until the early '70s to have radio communication was a rare luxury, and often signals between groups of rescuers on the hill and the rescue base were made by Very pistol, so that in bad weather communications were virtually non-existent. Nowadays the Home Office provides sufficient radio sets, through the police, for every MRT to have a hill-set for each operational group. Search and rescue bases are issued with a high-powered set and team leaders are issued with vehicle radios which can also be used as links in broken or hilly country. As well as rescue team groups, every SARDA handler on the call-out list has his own hill-set which he keeps on a permanent basis: most of them have a vehicle set as well.

There has always been very close co-operation between the police and MRTs. The police are the authority responsible for the safety of members of the public, and, if they receive information that someone is believed to be in difficulty, it is their job to seek the help of organisations such as the Coast Guard, RAF helicopters, or the Mountain Rescue services, whichever happens to be the appropriate group. In recent years the police have made much wider use of SARDA, thereby saving their own hard-pressed resources to a considerable extent. This aspect is covered fully in the following chapter, but there is no doubt that they set great store on our willingness 'to go anywhere, at any time, for no charge . . . ' and, to enable us to get into action with the least possible delay, they have recently issued the call-out co-ordinator with a 'bleeper' which is incorporated into the police traffic frequency. The routine is that if dogs are urgently required, the operations room at police HQ will first try to contact the SARDA call-out co-ordinator by telephone ('landline'); if this fails they will bleep him, and wherever he may be he will immediately contact control centre ('operations room') and take whatever action is necessary. A great deal of time and effort is saved in this way.

Searches today are all treated as emergencies, and the first priority is to look for clues, not the person. That means that you do not go dashing out onto the mountain until all the evidence has been gathered, and a logical plan of action has been thought out. Every person who might have spoken to the missing person must be questioned; his room or tent must be closely examined to see if he has left a guide-book or some other clue as to where he might have gone; someone must check and try to ascertain what equipment and clothing he has taken with him; and as a matter of routine the police will contact his home address. All this must be done immediately on receiving the information that someone is missing, and until it has been done, the first requirement of a search manager has not been completed. Every piece of information of any sort must be collected and considered urgently. This is the initial response and any delay is unacceptable, but it has not always been thus, as the early stories show.

The improvement in techniques in Britain has been based largely on facts and figures which have been compiled in America and, whilst in many respects conditions under which search and rescue operations are conducted in the United States are different from those in this country – especially as regards distances – and therefore their statistics are not always completely relevant, they are for the time being the only ones available. It will be several years before enough statistics are compiled by our own MR organisations to be able to make a worthwhile comparison with those we have obtained from America. It will make interesting reading when this can be done. For example, their figures show that 50% of fatalities occur within the first twenty-four hours of a person going missing and that another 24% succumb in the next twenty-four hours. In view of the geographical and climatic differences involved, can we assume that 74% of fatalities in Britain all happen in the first two days? It might be more, or it might be less. We shall have to wait and see. Those involved in MR are always striving to make their operation more professional on the premise that if it's worth doing at all, it's worth doing well. You will have seen from some of the stories how teams of searchers used to be committed to the hill with little or no information, and in one case did not even know the name of the man we were supposed to be looking for. The search parties went out, formed an extended line and carried out a sweep search often over very large areas. Sometimes, in the early stages of an operation, they would maintain distances between each person and barge through anything which happened to be in the way, such as clumps of brambles and gorse, and end up with torn equipment and clothing. Then, as the enthusiasm wore a bit thin and excitement gave way to boredom, such obstacles would be by-passed, so that progressively the area was being searched less and less efficiently. Nevertheless, by the law of averages, these methods were sometimes successful, but more by luck than good planning and judgement.

Today, however, with priority being given to the gathering of information, some of the more progressive MRTs are already using computers to record every piece of information they can find which might influence their planning. No longer is it acceptable for a team leader who receives a call from the police at any time after dark, for example, to call out a search party for 'first light' – possibly twelve hours later – and do nothing else in the meantime. The modern leader with professional ideas will hand over the job of telephoning his team members to someone else whilst he himself will meet the informant and talk to him so that gradually and methodically he will build up a picture of the missing person, and at the same time be starting to formulate his search plan. It is somewhat similar to 'Monty' in the Western Desert when he was fighting Rommel; he always had a photograph of his adversary in front of him so that he could try to read his mind and think what he would do next!

One of the trail-blazers in the quest for more professional techniques is the Ogwen Valley Mountain Rescue Organisation, or 'Oggie' as it is affectionately called. Dr Tony Jones, who was for many years their chairman, built up a close rapport with several SAR organisations in the United States and, with the more senior and experienced of his colleagues in 'Oggie', has adopted modern technology and methods of search management. They installed a computer and a 'FAX' machine, and the latter has already proved invaluable in immediately informing the Rescue Co-ordination Centre (RCC) at Pitreavie near Edinburgh of details of terrain over which a search is taking place, along with all relevant information about the search operation itself. This enables the RCC to assess the problem and decide on the need for more aircraft, for example.

'Oggie' was one of the first teams to realise that the organisation and running of a big search operation is not a one-man job, and, like most MRTs in Britain, they are now operating on the basis of a search management team made up of a number of members who have done the Search Management Course, and are competent to share in the running of the operation. In this way, right from the start, the best minds available are involved in the planning, and no stone is left unturned.

Search and Rescue Dogs

I first became interested in SARDA when I was navigating for Roland Layland on a search in Cwm Glas. He and I, with a large German Shepherd called Paddington, were working across the cwm, an extensive area of broken ground, with the RAF Valley MRT doing a follow-up sweep-search behind us. It was the first time I had seen a SARDA dog in action, and I was impressed with the amount of ground covered by the dog as Roland worked him to the edges of the designated search area; and as we worked into the wind, Roland explained the theory and practice of using dogs for this kind of search. I remember asking him why, if the dog was so good, it was necessary to have another twelve men following in our wake, which seemed to me to be a complete waste of our manpower resources. He answered that there was a great deal of prejudice against the concept and use of search dogs, and that, until they were accepted 'in high places' and by the teams, MR in general would be losing a most efficient and valuable means of searching for missing people in wilderness areas.

The Search and Rescue Dog Association, (SARDA), was formed in Scotland in 1965, and at first covered the whole of Britain. By 1971 it had become unwieldy and was divided into three autonomous associations, Scottish, English and Welsh. Its working parts are 'dog teams' – a handler and his dog; and today there are normally about ten such teams on the Welsh call-out list. They are ready for duty at any time and will go anywhere, even outside the principality, to help anyone, for no charge; thus ensuring a swift response by trained, skilled personnel whose Search and Rescue activities are usually their vocation.

A search is mounted when a casualty's location or physical condition is not known, or when there is reason to believe that someone is in difficulty and needs help, such as in the tragic story of 'SOS Unanswered' (chapter 28). The purpose of SARDA is to speed up the rescue of people missing on the hills and moors, by finding them more quickly. In this way SARDA will effectively help to save more lives, and minimise pain and suffering to anyone unfortunate enough to have an accident in some remote area. SARDA also helps the police by searching for missing people in open

Roland Layland's Toby homes in on the casualty. *Author*

Having returned to Roland, he brings him to his find, still indicating to his handler by barking. *Author*

After examining the casualty, Roland has called in the helicopter and, as it approaches, he lets off a smoke flare to indicate his position and the strength and direction of the wind.   *Author*

The helicopter has winched down a Thomas stretcher and MRT personnel, here seen with the stretchered casualty almost ready for a carry off.   *Author*

On their way down a steep slope. Note the safety back rope under tension.   *Author*

country anywhere, and these include young children or the elderly who wander away and get lost; quite often, too, the dogs are asked to look for people of all ages who have 'had enough' and go out to end it all.

All SARDA handlers are trained in advanced search techniques and are provided with all necessary equipment. They must be competent mountaineers, devoted to the training of their dogs and be prepared to venture on to the mountains at night and in bad weather. They must be active members of an MRT, and give a great deal of time to train for, and take part in, search and rescue operations; it is an entirely voluntary service, and handlers pay for the maintenance of their dogs, most of the rescue equipment, travelling expenses and all other costs, out of their own pockets. It is an expensive commitment, and all for the doubtful pleasure of often spending hours out on the hill in atrocious weather when the rest of the community is tucked up asleep in bed.

Before participating in searches with my dog, I spent a year studying all I could about training and working a search dog, attending monthly training exercises and lectures, (which included being used as an avalanche casualty buried under a metre of snow.) Throughout the year, I received tremendous help and encouragement from all the members of SARDA (Wales), in particular Roland, Phil Williams-Jones, Steve Mitchell and Chris Wharmby, all of whom were enthusiastic and highly skilled handlers.

The origin of SAR dogs goes back a long way, in fact as far as the 17th century and the legendary dogs of the famous St Bernard hospice in Switzerland. Dogs were brought to the hospice initially to serve as guards, but later began to accompany the monks on their missions to rescue travellers in difficulty. Then, in the First World War, dogs were trained by the Red Cross to locate wounded soldiers on the battlefield during a lull in the fighting. The dogs were trained to 'home-in' on the human scent emanating from the wounded men and, during the blitz in the Second World War, the same skills were utilised to find people buried under the rubble of bombed buildings. Today both the European and American rescue services train and maintain teams ready to be sent anywhere where disaster strikes, such as earthquakes, volcanic eruptions, and landslides.

After the Second World War, the Swiss Alpine Club began the training of dogs to locate avalanche victims in much the same way as they had been trained to find people under ruined buildings. In Britain, however, snow avalanches do not present the same problem, and in England and Wales it is the hill-walker or climber who goes missing in mist or driving rain, or at night, who presents the main difficulty. In many parts of Britain there are vast tracts of open moorland and mountains of over three thousand feet, under snow for a good part of the winter, where bad weather is normal.

To appreciate the value of a SAR dog, you must imagine searching over a vast expanse of snow-covered ground for someone who may have fallen exhausted or injured, and been covered by a blanket of snow or even hoar frost. Gazing over the white landscape, there is no indication of where the missing person might be, and this is where the sensitive nose of the search dog gives him such an advantage. When the dog crosses the band of human scent which is carried on the wind from the casualty – and this can be at a distance of up to five hundred metres or more in ideal conditions – the dog will 'alert' and indicate the direction in which the person is lying. He will then follow the scent upwind and, having located the casualty, will return to the handler and take him in to the position. It is the sensitive nose of the search dog, able to detect what the human eye cannot, which makes him equal to at least twenty human searchers in normal search conditions, i.e. at night or in bad visibility. The Press have great difficulty in distinguishing between SARDA and 'tracker dogs', and often the latter are credited in reports with successful searches which have been done by the former. Tracker dogs quite simply follow tracks along the ground, and are not trained to pick up and follow an air scent; on the other hand SARDA dogs

Chris Malyon approaches Teryn's find in deep snow.   *Paul Harris*

will first of all attempt to pick up an air scent, but if there is no wind and they detect a ground scent, they will certainly follow that. In effect, therefore, SAR dogs can and will carry out both types of search, whilst tracker dogs will normally only follow ground scent.

The first essential is clearly a good 'nose', or scenting ability, and usually the longer the dog's nose, the better it will be. Then he should be large enough and possess the stamina to negotiate difficult and variable terrain over long distances for many hours on end, often in deep snow conditions. Whether a dog has the stamina to make a good SAR dog will only become apparent as the animal develops. Very exceptionally a handler has to take his dog out of training when it becomes obvious that it is just not strong enough. The dog should ideally be fairly long in the leg, and have a long reach and fluid 'ground-eating' action; and of course he should have no hip displasia, arthritis or other disease. Medium-sized breeds such as the German Shepherd, Collie or Labrador are most popular. All of these are responsive to the specialised training and can make excellent SAR dogs. Crosses between these breeds probably produce the best of all worlds as they have hybrid vigour and are 'tougher' in every sense of the word.

Mark Windham building up essential rapport with his young dog.   *Richard Birch*

Before search training begins, the dog must have a good grounding in obedience, but not to the extent that he works only to command, as sometimes mistakenly happens. The SAR dog always works off the lead and is required to free-range well away from his handler with a minimum of interference and direction. That means that he must use plenty of initiative and think for himself. The ideal age at which to start search training is between six months and one year, but older dogs will sometimes respond to this sort of work and can achieve a high degree of efficiency. When training begins, the emphasis is on making a 'find', and the young dog soon learns to enjoy playing hide-and-seek with his handler, so that throughout his career as a SAR dog, a search is always a game to be enjoyed. When the dog has made his find, he is trained to return to his handler and indicate to him that there is a 'body' ahead. How the dog does this is either by barking or by his own particular method such as leaping excitedly up and down. Some dogs absolutely refuse to bark, and in spite of all the efforts of the North Wales Police dog handlers, Gwynne, my first search dog, only began to speak when she made a find just before I retired her!

'Complete empathy': John Gladstone and Stout.   *Gwyn Roberts*

Just before Christmas in 1978, I was given an eight-week-old bitch puppy – a crossed German Shepherd/Collie – by a Mrs Doreen Jones, The Butchers Shop, Aberffraw in Anglesey. This was an ideal cross, and I called her Gwynne. She was completely black apart from a white blaze down her chest. Like all puppies she was adorable, but my wife was not at all pleased with me for getting a puppy with the hotel fully booked for Christmas and New Year! But we managed to get by and avoided piddle-stained carpets with copious splashes of soda water to neutralise the acid.

Immediately after Christmas, I started her basic obedience training followed soon by initial search training in which my wife and children helped. Gwynne was a quick learner and we did a short period of training almost every day until she was ready to start more ambitious work in the mountains. I had a tremendous amount of fun throughout this period and, whilst training Gwynne, I was training myself as a handler: for dog and handler are one team, and the dog can only be as good as the handler, and vice versa. By early November 1979, it was suggested that it was time for Gwynne to be assessed as a novice dog. I had not even considered this as I wanted to be quite sure that we were good and ready before taking this step. I was persuaded that we were working so well together that we had a very good chance of passing the December assessment, and that, even if we failed, we would have gained a lot of experience.

The assessment was held in Cwm Eigiau in the Carneddau and there were six assessors – police sergeants Kenny McKenzie and Bill Meekie from Scotland, two from England, and two from Wales. All handlers become very tense when they go for assessment, as all the work put into training is going to be put to the test in one short day. We all strive desperately to get through: it is a matter of pride when we do and of intense disappointment when we are failed. But standards must be kept as high as possible, and if we fail, as I did on one occasion, it only makes you more determined to get through next time. I remember one young handler who was one of our keenest members, and who was failed after a year's hard graft. He was completely shattered and his tears showed the magnitude of his disappointment. But he has persevered and, during the time he was training a new dog, he never failed to go out as navigator to one of the other handlers. That, to me, shows complete dedication.

On the December assessment, conditions were ideal for searching and I was given an area of about a thousand square metres. We worked methodically up-wind, criss-crossing the ground and suddenly Gwynne was away, nose up and tail out behind, straight as a die into the wind to make her find in a small cluster of boulders. I was so pleased that I just stood and watched until she came back to tell me she had found, and then she took me in to the 'body'. When I proudly went back to Kenny and Bill, feeling that Gwynne had not put a foot wrong, the first question they asked was 'Why on earth I had just stood and watched? Surely I should have followed her in rather than wait for her to come all the way back to tell me?' It was a good point, and one I took to heart. On her next search I did precisely what they had told me, immediately I saw her go to the body. This satisfied the two assessors, and Gwynne was passed as a Novice dog. She was put on the call-out list and during the following twelve months she improved every time she went out and I became increasingly confident that she would pass her assessment to full search dog next time.

During the year following our successful novice assessment, I learned a great deal about the nature and sensitivity of dogs and came to realise how very like young children they really are! One incident in particular remains firmly implanted in my memory, and it happened during a training day in the Carneddau. Gwynne and I were searching an area with the right hand boundary running in a north-easterly direction along Cefn Tal-llyn-Eigiau. The wind was blowing strongly from due south, so that we were in the lee of the ridge where it was relatively calm and we were searching with, rather than into, the wind. Towards the end of the ridge we were working upwards when Gwynne appeared to pick up a vestige of scent. She wasn't really sure at first, and slowly followed it to the top of the ridge through a small saddle and disappeared from view. I hurried after her, and when I went through the saddle, all I could see was a small black dot streaking at full gallop across the slopes which dropped down to the northern end of Llyn Eigiau. She was fully 600 metres away when she disappeared into dead ground. Soon she reappeared, still running fast, and came right back to indicate that she had found a casualty. But I knew that she had been into another dog team's search area and rather than interrupt his exercise, I made a fuss of Gwynne but did not allow her to take me back to her find. She gave me a withering look and for the rest of the morning she absolutely refused to work or do anything I asked her to do. In fact she sulked and was in a very bad temper indeed – not without good reason, as I'd not played my part and gone back with her to see her find. At lunch time I was sick at heart for the poor dog, and to try to cheer her up and get her to snap out of her sulks, I gave her at least half my food on the premise that the quickest way to a dog's heart is through the stomach! I knew that it had worked, and we went off to have a bit of fun together which culminated in doing some small searches in which I knew she could not fail to find. It did not take long for Gwynne to regain her confidence in herself and, more importantly, in me and before the day's exercise ended we did one more extensive search successfully. It was typical of Gwynne that she would never stop trying to do her job, and I suppose that when I did not respond as I should have done to her 'find' indication, she just said to herself, 'Oh, what the hell, that's it then' and went into her sulk.

The year as a novice was just as hard work as the first, but we had the added bonus of some real, live searches. The first of these was on the Great Orme, at the eastern end of Llandudno Bay, when the Coastguards had been called out to look for an elderly gentleman who had gone for an evening walk and not returned home. The Chairman of the 'Oggie' team, Dr Tony Jones, had been asked to co-ordinate, and five dog-teams took part in the operation. We worked the cliff tops and further inland until the small hours and, although we did not find the old man, one of the dogs did in fact give a very strong indication, repeated by another dog, from a point directly above a rocky beach. This was reported to the RNLI and, at first light, the inshore lifeboat went out to scan the foot of the cliffs and found the missing man lying on the rocks where he had fallen to his death the previous evening. The indication given by the dog proved to be entirely accurate. I was very satisfied with the way Gwynne had worked and, before leaving the area for home, was given a personal radio. I was very pleased about this for it was a mark of confidence in our ability as a SARDA team.

SARDA handlers are the only individuals in MR, apart from team leaders, who are issued with their own radios. On a rescue, only team or group leaders carry sets, but SARDA handlers always operate on their own and have their own radios so that, when there is a call-out, they do not waste valuable time making a detour to a MRT base to collect a team set. Since they are alone on the mountain, the radio is their only means of communication, so that, if they make a find or are unlucky enough to have an accident themselves, they can summon help. A handler will therefore look after his set in his own interest and make sure it is always in good working order with batteries kept charged. After the extra year's experience together, Gwynne and I attended the assessment course for up-grading in December 1980, and passed with no problem at all. It was a proud moment in which all my family joined and all the time, effort, patience and expense had finally paid off.

As SARDA became more credible and were being called out more frequently, we began to feel that at last we were in sight of winning our battle for recognition. In fact in 1985, including MRT call-outs, I attended no

Tony Jones (left), President of SARDA (Wales), and Bob Maslen-Jones, watching a SARDA exercise. Gwyn Roberts

fewer than twenty-five incidents, an average of one every two weeks. It was one thing for SARDA to be affiliated to the Mountain Rescue Committee, but quite another for MRTs to accept that a good, well-trained SARDA team was the equivalent of no less than twenty human searchers. We were determined not to lose our hard-won reputation as the most important weapon in the search manager's armoury. Training exercises were carried out every month, standards of performance constantly vetted, and during the winter we organised evening classes once a fortnight to study search techniques, the effect of wind, weather and terrain on the behaviour of scent, and so on. As amateurs we were steadily becoming more professional at our job and it was always stressed that one bad search, in which a casualty was 'missed' by a dog and the area wrongly declared clear, would undo all the hard work of years and do untold harm to our image.

As part of our training schedule we have spent a week in the Cairngorms every March since 1980, when SARDA (Wales) took on the responsibility from Tom Redfern with whom I had done two such courses before he handed over to Roland Layland. Tom Redfern's courses were fun, but you had to be pretty hardy to cope with the Norwegian Hostel near Loch

Heather Maling, one of the few female MRT members. She was a dog-handler with SARDA (Wales) during the working life of two dogs – Bramble, and her offspring, Spruce, who was Gelert's little sister. Heather is now training to be a physiotherapist in Birmingham.

Morlich! It was a vast building with little to commend it in the way of home comforts. It was cold and draughty and food was basic. Not surprisingly, only twenty stalwart handlers and 'dogs bodies' (volunteer casualties) took time off to go. Nevertheless the training was valuable and when the hostel was bought by the Army, we had to look elsewhere.

I knew of Clive and Sally Freshwater's 'Cairngorm Canoe and Sailing School' at Insh Hall, Kincraig, because my two sons had been taught to canoe and sail there, and I thought it had good possibilities. Clive and Sally were prepared to accommodate us and put up with twenty or so dogs, all of which would be kept in their handlers' vehicles. The first course was held at Insh in 1981 when Heather Maling took over the catering at very short notice, and it was voted a success. There are excellent training areas down Glen Feshie and up in the northern corries of the Cairngorms, and we booked again for 1982. Heather did not want to do another course, and I was rash enough to offer to be the course organiser, which included the catering and accommodation, and duty rosters. Surprisingly Clive and Sally were glad to have us back again, and year by year the week has become more and more popular. We have had to put a limit on numbers, and the first fifty-four

Neil Rawlinson (left) and Dave Williams with their dogs Wilfie and Shem during a pause in a training exercise.   *Richard Birch*

who apply are the lucky ones.

After organising the course for eight years during which my wife took on the responsibility for catering, we gracefully retired and Heather Maling once again took over for one year. It is now run by Neil Rawlinson.

There can be no doubt that this training week has proved to be very valuable, as it provides the opportunity for handlers from the Welsh and English SARDAs, and sometimes one or two from the Borders and Highlands, to discuss all sorts of problems and training techniques to their mutual advantage. Many 'old hands' come on the course to help with the training, but apart from the serious side it is a great social gathering of people who are committed to doing a worthwhile job with SARDA.

There are several other aspects of SARDA training and probably the most important of these is preparing for the stock test. This has to be done from the very earliest days, otherwise if a dog shows an interest in stock after months of search training, it will all have been a complete waste of time. By then it will be far more difficult to get the dog to ignore other animals and it will almost certainly result in the dog being taken out of training altogether. The behaviour of dogs, especially among sheep, is critical, as a search dog must never be distracted when working and, what is probably equally important, he must be seen by the farming community not to be a menace to their livestock. SARDA is dependent on the goodwill of sheep farmers to allow training exercises to be carried out on their land, which they will only do when they have complete confidence in the handlers' control of their dogs, even when they are out of sight. In fact, no dog is allowed to take part in a training search exercise until it has been stock-tested by a local sheep farmer; and their standards are very severe.

From time to time a shepherd or farmer proves to be utterly obdurate and will not give permission for training on his land. Their warnings must be taken seriously as in practice it is a question of shoot first and make excuses afterwards. It is understandable in areas where large numbers of casual walkers take their dogs with them without realising the damage their animals can do if they are not kept strictly under control. After all, the walkers are there to enjoy themselves, but not at the expense of the farmer's livelihood.

One such man, Gilbert Jones, who was the shepherd on the Vaynol Estate, whose land runs up to the summit of Snowdon astride the railway track, was resolute in his refusal to allow us to work our dogs there. He was always polite, but firm, and he explained that the path running up the valley was one of the most popular routes to Snowdon and it was impossible to know which dogs were under training and which were likely to take off and run the sheep.

The stock test.   *Paul Harris*

No amount of persuasion would make him change his mind until one night there was a call-out to look for a small boy who had gone missing from his home not far from Port Dinorwic on the Menai Strait. Several dog teams were involved over a wide area, as there was no indication as to where the boy might have gone. After three hours one of the dogs found him curled up asleep under a tree, and it then turned out that he was Gilbert's son. From that moment, nothing was too much trouble for him, and he was delighted when we asked him if he would carry out the stock test at the next assessment. It was always a pleasure to train on Gilbert's land after that, but when the estate was sold we lost touch with him. The new farmer took the same line that Gilbert had done before we found his small son, and in spite of having some interesting and lengthy discussions, he is immovable! Happily there are many hill farmers who realise the value of the work SARDA does, and as one remarked, "Well, I might be the next victim you have to look for, mightn't I?"

Although Gwynne had passed her stock tests at intervals, I was always aware that she did in fact have a lively interest in sheep and it was a constant struggle to persuade her that her role in life was to search for human beings, and not to round up sheep! Within a few weeks of passing her assessment to full search dog, we were in Scotland assessing the Scottish Highlands dogs, and on the first day I was helping a local hill sheep farmer to carry out the stock test on his farm at the bottom of the Pass of Glencoe. Throughout the morning Gwynne had lain at my feet watching every movement the sheep made. When it was all over the farmer said "How much will you take for your dog?" "Not for sale," I replied, "I've just spent two years training her with my family, and I'm not selling." "Go on, name your price," he went on, "She's got a wonderful eye for the sheep, and she's a big strong bitch, just the job for hill work round here. I want her, and I'll give you what you ask." "I'm sorry, but I cannot sell her. After all the work we have done together to train her as a search dog, the family would never forgive me." The conversation ended, but I have often thought about it, and as things turned out later, I think that perhaps Gwynne might have had a more fulfilling life up there in the mountains around Glencoe than she did as a search dog in Snowdonia.

Within a year or so, the innate instinct to eye the sheep which was so apparent in Glencoe had begun to dominate, and I seriously started to doubt whether I could fully trust her to stay on a search pattern if there were any sheep about. The problem was solved for me when we were on a training exercise in Cwm Bychan, near the start of the Roman Steps in the Rhinog hills inland from Harlech. All the handlers and 'bodies' were standing in the carpark watching Roland Layland working his GSD Toby on the hill immediately to the north when Gwynne brought half a dozen ewes she had rounded up into the carpark, right in front of everyone. The gaff was blown as they all saw what she had done, and there was no way I could offer a sufficiently plausible and acceptable excuse. I knew the rules and sadly I had to take Gwynne out of training, and she went into retirement. I was naturally very upset about it, but by this time I had another dog ready to replace Gwynne, of which more later. Gwynne's retirement was anything but quiet, and of course she always came out with me and Gelert on the mountains. It was on two of these walks that what she had done in the carpark at Cwm Bychan proved to be just the tip of an iceberg! She had never been trained to round up sheep, neither had she ever lived with working sheepdogs. The only time I had tried to teach her to move sheep was when a ewe with lamb at foot had come into the grounds of our house at Waunfawr, but that was long after she had been retired. The first incident happened in Cwm Eigiau when, after a morning's exercise, we had all gathered at Eigiau cottage for lunch. The local farmer was bringing his sheep up the Cwm to fold them in a large stone-walled pen, just a few yards in front of the cottage. His three dogs were working the sheep up and he was standing by the open gate ready to close it when all the sheep were inside the pen. As the first sheep ran through the gate, a group of six or seven broke away and ran down the hill by the stone wall, only to be turned back and brought back up to the gate by one of the dogs. As soon as he had all the animals inside, the farmer came over and said "and who do I have to thank for that?" "What do you mean?" someone asked. "I only had three dogs," he answered. "Now there are four, and that one, (pointing at the dog which had turned the breakaway group back) isn't one of them." I looked and suddenly realised it was Gwynne, whom I had taken with me on the exercise although I was working my other dog, Gelert. What she had done was pure instinct, and my mind harked back to the stock test in Glencoe. That farmer was a shrewd judge! The second indicent happened in 1990 on the Scottish course when a group of us walked from Glenmore Lodge over Bynack More. It was misty on top and Gwynne had wandered off into the fog away to our right. I was not concerned as it was a vast open area and there were no sheep about. But after ten minutes or so there was a noise like distant thunder which quickly changed to galloping hooves as a dozen reindeer came charging out of the mist with Gwynne proudly running along after them, her job of rounding them up complete. The two incidents show that however hard you may try, a dog's instinct, if sufficiently strong, will defeat all your efforts to eliminate it.

Gwynne had another very strong instinct – an aversion to the opposite sex. She seemed to hate dogs, and the Vet opined that her hormones must have been somewhat mixed up at birth. She resolutely resisted the attentions of dogs I had chosen to be her mate and whatever we did, she would have none of it. Until, that is, she was caught unawares in the hotel garden by a nondescript marauding village dog. In due course she produced an equally nondescript litter of eight puppies. I managed to find homes for all of them, but only one looked and behaved anything like Gwynne, and later on, when the owner suggested that we might breed from her using Gelert as stud, she too refused to submit.

Gwynne's litter was weaned just a week before we went up to Insh Hall for the Scottish training week, and I soon realised that she was far from being mountain fit. On the first day of the course, Denise Barley, a member of SARDA (Highlands) and the Cairngorm MRT, organised an exercise for us in the corries to the East of Glen Feshie. There was a foot of level snow lying over heather, and a very strong, almost gale force wind blew throughout the day from the south-west. Gwynne and I were given four hours to locate the casualty in our area, which covered approximately three square kilometres, but after quartering the windward slopes of the corrie we were both exhausted; Gwynne had completely lost all interest and she just plodded along a few feet behind me. I realised then that I had seriously underestimated the debilitating effects of rearing her litter. I scoured the leeward slopes with my binoculars, but nowhere could I see any sign of any disturbed snow and I was doubtful if, in fact, there was a casualty in the area at all. I decided therefore to call it a day as we were achieving precisely nothing, and I told Gwynne that we would walk down the stream to the end of the search area and then walk back to the vehicles along the route we had followed earlier in the day. She immediately understood what I was saying and trotted off several yards ahead of me. Of course dogs don't understand actual words, but they do pick up the meaning of what you say to them, and Gwynne wasted no time in agreeing with my decision.

We were just 50 metres from the stream junction where we had entered the area when Gwynne suddenly alerted, facing into the wind towards the ridge which was some 300 metres above us. She sniffed the wind for a few moments then looked at me with both a message and a question in her eyes – 'there's a definite scent; shall I go?' It had been a frustrating search until then, and deep snow lying over lush heather is not the easiest surface to walk over. I thought that Gwynne might follow the scent for a short distance and then run out of steam and come back to me. "Go on then," I said, "Go find him," and she was away. She ran straight up the slope for about 250 metres, nose up and tail out behind, and then she turned half left running diagonally upwards across the slope to the far skyline, where she appeared to lose the scent. I signalled her with my arm to go upwards, which she did and shortly went out of sight over the top of the ridge. Meantime I realised that Gwynne was not going to come back as I had hoped, and I set off up the hill heading for the spot where she had disappeared over the ridge skyline. About half-way up the slope, I found myself crossing an obvious shoulder which was probably the 'point of tension' for an avalanche to start. Already there were some cracks appearing along the contour and I went very carefully to avoid triggering an avalanche. To my horror Gwynne suddenly re-appeared galloping fast down the hill towards me and my immediate thought was that if anything was going to start the snow moving it was going to be her. She came to a four point halt, all four legs splayed out as she sent a cloud of snow over me. She was wild with excitement and indicated in every way possible that she had found our body, and when I told her "Good girl, show me then, show me," she turned and ran back to the ridge to where the body was lying. I made my best speed in her wake, but with already tired legs my progress was rather slow, and once more before I reached the ridge Gwynne had come down to indicate her find and tell me to hurry up! Eventually I joined her just over the ridge where our casualty was some three feet down a snow hole. Both Gwynne and I were over the moon with this find for it was certainly by far the longest strike I had ever seen, and in view of her condition, tiredness and lack of interest for the past two hours, it really was an amazing effort. When I got back to Insh Hall, I carefully and accurately measured on the 1:25,000 map, the distance from the valley bottom to the casualty, along the route she had followed, and it was a little over 1500 metres with an ascent of 300 metres. The normal distance for a search dog to strike is up to 500 metres, but on several occasions our dogs have followed scent to a casualty in excess of that.

As the week drew towards its close Gwynne did not seem to be herself at all. She lost her appetite, showed no interest in training and told me with her eyes that she was a sick dog, and I was rather worried about her. I did not take her out again, and when we got home to Llanberis, I took her to my then Vet, a Mr Jones, who was as baffled as I was. Gwynne did not respond to antibiotics or any other treatment, and as by now I feared that I was going to lose her, I insisted to Mr Jones that he should open her up and see what the cause of the infection was. For infection there must be as there was a nasty urethral discharge and I had convinced myself that her womb had turned

SAR dog Gwynne makes a find during the annual avalanche training week in the Cairngorms.   *Author*

septic. Mr Jones eventually agreed and when I went to collect Gwynne, he told me that he had had to perform a hysterectomy on her as there were two dead puppies stuck in the neck of the womb which had putrified. He added, somewhat to my amusement, that "If 'we' hadn't decided to operate, she wouldn't have lasted another day." Gwynne quickly recovered and it was not long before I had her back in training and fully mountain fit again. But it all made that 1500 metre strike all the more remarkable!

During the summer of 1981, Heather Maling's Labrador bitch, Bramble, was crossed by Roger Pyve's Labrador × Weimeraner, Dusty. She was due to pup one afternoon when Heather could not be with her and she asked me to look in and ensure that all was well. I found Bramble just starting and I stayed with her until all the pups had been safely born. I had been thinking of getting another dog to train and, when Heather offered me the pick of the litter, I chose an all-black, dog pup which I had particularly noticed as being strong and lively from the moment he arrived. He turned out just as I expected – not quite as thick-set as the pure Labrador and slightly longer in the leg; but above all he has a quiet, affectionate temperament and is a great companion. So Gelert joined the family circle and, once again, the training cycle started. Like Gwynne he was an exceptionally quick learner and passed his novice assessment after one year's work, being up-graded to full search dog twelve months later. Gelert developed into a first-class search dog, always keen to get out on the hill and anxious to please.

In the early Spring of 1985 we spotted a notice about a competition in the *Sunday Express* Colour Magazine, joint sponsors being Sherleys Pet Care Products. It was agreed that Gelert would do a complete search sequence which would be videoed and the tape sent to London for the six judges to see. We were lucky to have a local policeman, Terry Jackson, who knew all about SARDA and the MR scene, and who was also a very keen video enthusiast. He had a wealth of expensive equipment and, although it took several days to complete the film because of bad weather, the end result was most satisfactory.

Eventually Gelert was declared the winner after a very close-run final, and the well-known dog behaviourist, Roger Mugford, declared "His training is modest, but it's his thinking round the problem which is impressive." *The Sunday Express* 'Country Vet', Brian Watkins, added "If we were looking for initiative, then it had to be Gelert. And of course someone out there on the mountains this summer may be saved, thanks to his work." As I stressed at the time, the same comments would have applied to any of our well-trained dogs.

Roger Pyves and Dusty being winched into the helicopter.   *Roland Layland*

During SAR operations it is often expedient for teams to be airlifted by RAF helicopters to distant locations, thus saving many hours of walking-in and thereby speeding up the finding and rescuing of missing or injured people. Dogs are introduced to the helicopter as early in their training as possible, even if they have to be carried in the handler's arms, and very soon they become accustomed to entering the aircraft on the ground with the engines running and rotors swirling round above them. In fact they actually start to look forward to riding in the 'chopper' and quite often, when we have been out walking, they hear the distinctive noise and watch the machine, longingly, as it flies past.

The dogs are also trained to be winched into and out of the helicopters with their handlers as it is frequently not possible for them to land in the mountains. It usually takes only one or two winches before the dog is perfectly calm and happy to be put into his special winching harness, hooked on to the cable and held firmly by the handler to give him reassurance. This type of training is on-going as the helicopter crews are rotated, but it does not take long for the excellent rapport between SARDA and the RAF to be re-established. We have always been most grateful for the unstinting co-operation we have received over the years, both in training and on search operations.

Search dog work can only be as good as individual teams, i.e. the handler

Peter Durst (SARDA England) sends his dog, Jan, away to begin his search.   *Keith Brown*

Jed Stone and Tomos. Jed is currently secretary of SARDA (Wales).   Gwyn Roberts

and his dog. The team trains, works and lives together, the search dog being an ordinary family pet when not on duty, who loves people and enjoys his work. All training is based on praise and reward incentive rather than on pain avoidance, which preserves the dog's high regard for human beings. The search dog team represents a life-time partnership requiring the finest rapport between man and dog. As soon as a dog-team has been put on the SARDA call-out list, it is attached to the handler's own MRT with which it will principally work. But as often as not, because there are so few dog-teams in Wales, all of them are called out to support whichever MRT happens to be running a particular search operation. They are also ready to assist local police forces in searching for missing people anywhere, whether it be at sea level or in the hills, anywhere in Wales or indeed anywhere in Britain. We have even been called to search for a lost walker in the south-west of the Irish Republic.

Probably the first of these non-mountain searches occurred in April 1982 when a local doctor went missing in his canoe in the estuary of the Afon Glaslyn, off Porthmadog. He was an experienced canoeist, skier and climber, and had left his home at Borth-y-Gest at 10.00 a.m. for a two hour trip. When he had not returned by 3.00 p.m., three hours overdue, the police

Jim Davies and Jack.   *Gwyn Roberts.*

were informed, and the Coastguard, Inshore lifeboat crew and C flight, RAF SAR helicopters were called in to help. At 8.00 p.m., the helicopter crew spotted the canoe, floating upside down out to sea north west of Harlech, and SARDA was called out. It was felt that the doctor might have struggled ashore and be lying injured or suffering from hypothermia anywhere round the estuary. Every dog on the call-out list took part in the operation and, throughout the night, they searched the sand-dunes and beaches from Black Rock, near Criccieth, to Harlech. The twelve dog teams started at 9.00 p.m. and were withdrawn to rest at 4.00 a.m. – a seven hour stint.

The doctor was not found, but at about midnight, Heather Maling's bitch Bramble, working northwards from Harlech along the high-water line, gave a positive indication of someone out to sea in the area where the canoe had been seen by the helicopter just before dark. Bramble picked up a scent blowing off the sea, turned into the wind and followed the scent until she was beaten back by the surf. The Coastguard was informed, and they worked out that if it was a body out there, it would drift south-west on the tide and would then be brought back inshore towards Shell Island at around first light. An inshore lifeboat and the helicopter started searching again at dawn, and within a few minutes the doctor's body was found and recovered from the sea. The tides and time were such that Bramble's indication was without doubt the position of the body at midnight.

Two months before this sea-level search, an RAF Harrier had disappeared from the radar screen shortly after turning south over Queensferry. Five SAR helicopters and RAF MRTs spent five hours scouring the landscape for the missing aircraft and its pilot until darkness fell, when SARDA was called out to continue the operation during the night. The dogs were given the task of searching the Clocaenog Forest, between Ruthin and Corwen. It was a very extensive and densely wooded area, and an aircraft could easily have crashed in the middle of it and been invisible from only a few metres away. We searched for most of the night but found no sign of the machine, nor any smell of spilled fuel, and we were withdrawn to rest in a drill hall in Corwen at 4.00 a.m. At first light we were re-deployed into the hills south of the A5 road and were joined by search parties from all the North Wales civilian and RAF MRTs. The remains of the plane, which had crashed into a re-entrant, were found at about 11.00 a.m. several miles from the road.

A letter of thanks was received from the Group Captain at Headquarters, Northern Maritime Air Region in Scotland, which read:–

On behalf of the Air Commander, Air Vice Marshal D C A Lloyd and all the Operation Staff here at Pitreavie, I write to thank you and the seven dog handlers of the SARDA who responded so promptly and efficiently in the search for the missing Harrier pilot on 12 & 13 February.

I was particularly impressed with the speed with which you searched the Clocaenog Forest. This was a vital part of the search which had to be conducted since the forest was a high probability area.

Without the dogs it would have been a long and tedious task indeed.

As a newcomer to the Edinburgh Rescue Co-ordination Centre I look forward to future co-operation between your Association and RAF rescue units under happier circumstances. Thank you again for all your help.

We were delighted to receive such a letter which was another step forward in our efforts to get what we saw as our well-deserved recognition. The following year a party of sixteen handlers and 'dogs bodies' from SARDA (Wales) visited the RCC on our way home after the annual course at Insh Hall, and were given a very warm welcome.

It is not only out-door activists or pilots who disappear on the mountains, and one of the most unpleasant operations in which SARDA has been involved occurred in early September 1982. A farmer's wife had been savagely hacked to death in their farmhouse near Harlech, and their nineteen-year-old son had immediately gone missing. The police were anxious to find and interview the man as quickly as possible and a large force of police officers with their 'tracker' dogs, an RAF helicopter and the RNLI inshore lifeboat were immediately involved in looking for him. SARDA was asked for all the dogs it could muster and although this was certainly not in our 'terms of reference', every handler rallied to the call and we were deployed to search the forests in the coastal strip, and up into the Rhinog mountains. It was not until three weeks later, when we were doing a follow-up search in the forests, that he was flushed out and made a run for it back to the farmhouse where he was promptly arrested.

Then, in January 1983 a massive hunt was launched for a forty-one-year-old patient from the psychiatric hospital at Llanfairfechan, mid-way between Bangor and Conwy. This 'timid man who had the mental age of a young child' and suffered from epilepsy, walked out of the hospital one afternoon and disappeared into thin air. He was said to be friendly and harmless, and a strong walker, but the only clue, which was somewhat tenuous, was that he had been seen heading out of the village into the northern hills of the Carneddau towards Tal-y-Fan. During the first night the weather was fairly bad; it was cold with snow showers, and all the available dog teams searched the beaches, caravan parks, quarries and mountains, but there was no sign of him. Next morning the 'Oggie', Llanberis and Clwyd teams were deployed over a very wide area, supported by the RAF Valley MRT and an overflying helicopter. After two days the search was scaled down and finally abandoned.

Three months later, a fell runner out on a training run lost his way in thick mist on the plateau north of Tal-y-Fan, and found himself heading into some very wet, soft bog. As he started to 'pound' his way back on to firmer ground, he could feel it shaking under his feet, and suddenly a skeleton popped up out of the bog right in front of him. The poor man nearly died of fright and beat a very hasty and panicky retreat from this awful spectre, to report what he had seen to the police. The skeleton was identified as the remains of the missing patient, and the only rational explanation of what had happened was that he must have walked on to the hill, blundered into the bog, and been sucked down into it as he struggled to get back on to firm ground. Certainly the SAR dogs had been all round the bog area more than once, as had MRT search parties, but as the body was by then well beneath the surface, nothing was either scented or seen.

There have been several searches for small children, and it must be said that whenever there is an incident involving 'kids' all the stops are pulled out and no effort is spared to find and recover them quickly. Such searches are usually very emotive from the start, especially when the distraught parents are around. You just do not feel adequate somehow and all you can do is go on searching until you get a result. Sadly, most of these searches end in us finding the child drowned in a ditch, disused septic tank, old pit shaft or the like, almost always close to home.

In the summer of 1988, a worried father reported that his six-year-old son had disappeared from their 'patch' on Newborough Beach on Anglesey. Not one of the hordes of holidaymakers had seen him wander off, though he was dressed in a distinctive green and black shirt and scarlet shorts. Within an hour the search dogs were on their way and the RAF Valley MRT was flown in by helicopter which then methodically overflew the forest, up and down the rides at low level; but nothing was seen. A Coastguard Land-rover patrolled up and down the beach until about 5.00 p.m., and was just going to turn round and call it a day when, way down towards Newborough Warren, beyond the edge of the forest, he saw the child emerge on to the beach, He had wandered through the trees for over a mile before he found himself in open ground.

I particularly remember this incident because of the attitude of the father. He was a rather aggressive thirty-year-old Midlander who had constantly criticised the rescue services for "being so slow and unconcerned." We tried to explain the set-up to him, and when it was all over he made a point of apologising, and he thanked everyone profusely; "Now I think about it," he said, "it's amazing how quickly, and how many, people responded to the call." This was very true; it was one of the slickest turn-outs I had yet seen.

Shortly before this incident, the ICI explosives factory at Penrhyndeudraeth blew up, scattering debris over a wide area. We were immediately asked to help in the search for two men who had been in the mixing room when the explosion occurred. It seemed obvious to us that we would not be looking for two men, but rather their remains and, although we had not trained the dogs to search for 'bits and pieces', we decided to make the effort. The four dogs involved showed remarkable versatility and within a few minutes they adapted to the painstakingly slow 'fine search' which was required. The task was gruesome and upsetting for the handlers, but the dogs found enough pieces for the pathologist to put together one of the missing men. 'Alerts' by the dogs indicated the whereabouts of the second man buried under the rubble.

Only six months later the Lockerbie air disaster happened. Bill Parr, the Chairman of the SARDA (Borders), happened to live in Lockerbie and,

ROYAL SOCIETY FOR THE PREVENTION OF CRUELTY TO ANIMALS

CERTIFICATE OF
COMMENDATION

Presented to

Search and Rescue Dog Association

by the Council in recognition of

the dedication and perseverance shown by the Association's Handlers and Dogs at the scene of the Lockerbie Aircraft Disaster. December 1988.

A. C. W. Hart

Chairman RSPCA Council

DATED THIS **3rd** DAY OF **May** 19**89**.

aware of the success of the search after the explosion in North Wales, he confidently offered the use of SARDA to the police. Dog teams from the Scottish Borders, England, Northern Ireland and Wales took part in the huge operation, and altogether 47 handlers and 51 dogs joined the search for bodies, personal items and parts of the plane over hundreds of square miles. The full story has been told elsewhere, but it is on record that the dog teams found one hundred and thirty-nine bodies and innumerable items such as wallets, clothing, suitcases and vital clues as to the cause of the crash. They earned a special 'Thank you' from the police directing the search. In this operation, seven dog teams from Wales went to Lockerbie in two shifts, so that we would always have at least two teams available on our home ground. For his part in the operation Bill Parr was awarded a well-deserved MBE, and the RSPCA gave every dog which took part a specially inscribed medallion, and each handler a copy of the Certificate of Commendation which they had awarded to the Search and Rescue Dog Association.

The use of search dogs in disaster areas such as earthquakes, volcanic eruptions (Mount St Helens) and large explosions has become widespread and most European countries, the USA and Canada train and maintain special SAR units in readiness to go anywhere in the world where such a disaster occurs. In October 1986, we received an urgent request from International Rescue to send two dog teams to join the British Rescue team in the earthquake disaster in El Salvador. We had, in fact, previously considered the possibility of doing the same thing, but our decision was that we should maintain our primary role of providing dog teams to work in Wales. In the sudden event, however, there were three handlers who were prepared to go out to El Salvador, and they all duly arrived in London ready to be flown out. When it was made clear that on their return all the dogs would have to be put into quarantine for six months, two of the three remembered their first responsibility, and dropped out. One handler, however, together with another from England, was flown out and within two hours of arriving they were working alongside dog teams from Switzerland, France and USA. With no specialised training for this kind of work, and in spite of unaccustomed heat and the all-pervading stench of corpses, the dogs quickly adapted and carried out their work most efficiently, once again proving their great versatility. The part they played, including locating a man who had been buried for nine days and was rescued alive, was highly praised by everyone concerned.

On return, as expected, the dogs went into quarantine for six months and, apart from the trauma of being parted from their handlers and being locked up for such a long time – which for an active animal is quite unacceptable – both Associations were denied the use of these dogs for up to nine months. After release from quarantine, it took an extra three months to get them mountain fit again. And of course the cost of quarantine at that time was £1,000 per dog! SARDA (Wales) then made a firm decision not to be involved in overseas operations, and this decision was fully justified in December 1988 when a huge earthquake devastated Armenia. There were plenty of properly trained SAR dogs available from countries which do not have Rabies quarantine laws, and one or two dog teams from Britain would have made little difference. Had we sent any of our dogs to Armenia, they would not have been available to take part in the Lockerbie search.

Over the years, Gelert and Gwynne had become the best of friends, and Gwynne could not understand why, on training days or on operational searches, she had to be left in the car. I tried to make up for these disappointments by making a bit more of a fuss of her, but it was always pitiful to hear her howls when I walked away with Gelert. Once she had been retired, she became a devoted companion, and it was a sad day in 1989 when she developed a problem which did not show any sign of responding to treatment in spite of all the efforts of Neil and Gill Hubbard, our Association's honorary Veterinary Officers from Caernarfon. It was obvious to me that she was rapidly losing the quality of life to which she was entitled and, in the early autumn, I was faced with the dreadful decision to ask Neil to put her to sleep. I held her in my arms as her eyes slowly closed and twelve years of a loving relationship had ended. Neil was very supportive, but I only just managed to get out of the surgery before my grief got the better of me and I wept for Gwynne.

When I got into the car, Gelert knew exactly what I had done. He sat, head bowed, with the most pathetic look on his face, and this made my sadness even worse. It was several days before Gelert came to terms with the fact that Gwynne had gone; he was listless and off his food, but I knew that I had made the right decision for Gwynne, even if Gelert and I felt her going so acutely. I still miss Gwynne when I am out walking with Gelert, but am sure she is happy, romping round in her 'doggy heaven'. Gelert, now past his twelfth birthday, grows old gracefully; a little grey round his muzzle perhaps, and showing signs of stiffness now and then, but still the same lovable character which endears him to everyone he meets.

INDEX

Bob Maslen-Jones was born in Wolverhampton in 1921, and was educated at Oundle and New College, Oxford.

Prep school on the Malvern Hills, camps in the Welsh mountains and high-level treks in the Austrian Tyrol and Swiss Alps instilled in him his life-long love of mountaineering.

During almost fifteen years in the Army, he climbed mountains in Kurdistan, the Lebanon, Northern Iran, Kashmir and the Troodos.

In civilian life he served on the Council of the National Association of Boys' Clubs, and monthly expeditions to Snowdonia, the annual NABC Roof of Wales trek, and the Mountain Leadership Certificate in 1968, were steps along the way.

In 1975 Bob and his wife, Anne, bought a hotel in Llanberis, and he joined the Rescue Team. His ultimate, voluntary, career in MR had begun.

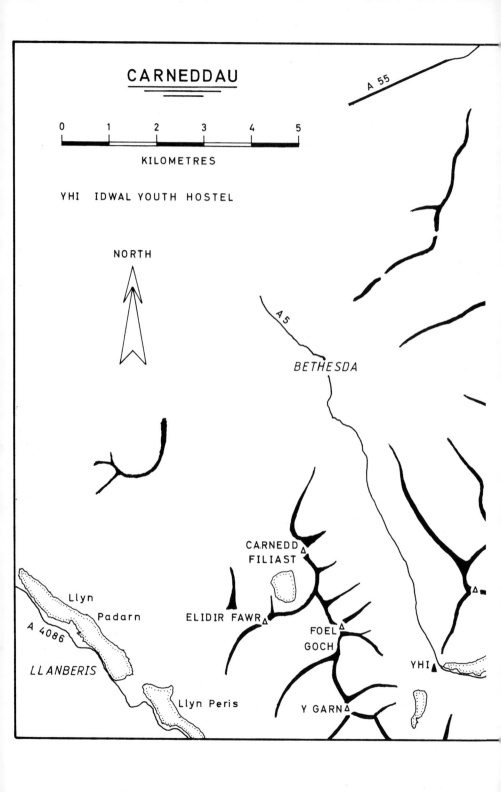